PRINCIPLES AND APPLICATIONS OF

Information Science

FOR LIBRARY PROFESSIONALS

John N. Olsgaard, editor

American Library Association
Chicago and London 1989

Designed by Herb Slobin
Cover design by Stephanie Torrell
Text prepared by ALA Books, using a BestInfo Wave4 pre-press system and output to a Linotronic L500 by Glenbard Graphics
Printed on 50-pound Glatfelter B-31, a pH-neutral paper, by Versa Press

The paper used in this publication meets the minimum requirements of American National Standard for Information Sciences—Permanence of Paper for Printed Library Materials, ANSI Z39.48–1984. ∞

Library of Congress Cataloging-in-Publication Data
Principles and applications of information science for library professionals / edited by John N. Olsgaard.
    p. cm.
    Includes index.
    ISBN 0–8389–0507–2 (alk. paper)
    1. Information science.   2. Information retrieval.   3. Information technology.   4. Libraries—Automation.   I. Olsgaard, John N.
Z665.P94 1989
020—dc19   88–36876

5 4 3 2 1   93 92 91 90 89

Contents

Figures

Introduction

John N. Olsgaard

To most library practitioners the term "information science" merely implies the application of computers to existing library-related operations. This characterization was partially inspired by some schools of library and information science that added "information science" to their names without significantly adding to their curriculum. As a result, a large portion of the library profession is without the terminology, concepts, and theory necessary to understand the developing discipline of information science, or its possible implications to the profession.

In his book *The Two Cultures*, C. P. Snow describes the story of a nineteenth-century literary intellectual who was a guest for dinner at Cambridge University. The literary intellectual tried to strike up a conversation with the professors seated around him, but got only grunts in reply. The Vice-Master at the table, having taken notice of the situation, said to the guest, "Oh, those are mathematicians! We never talk to *them*."[1] Snow went on to describe the widening gulf between intellectuals in the natural sciences and those in the humanities. Many of us in the business of teaching have seen a similar gulf developing between information scientists on one side and librarians on the other.

The focus of this book is on bridging this gulf, by delineating some of the more basic concepts of the discipline of information science. The book is written for, and directed toward, the practicing librarian. The assumption is made that the reader has little or no background in information science. It is hoped that once the reader has finished this volume, he or she will understand not only the overall direction and many of the basic concepts of information science, but also how information science principles might be applied in the professional environment.

This is not a "cutting-edge" book. The writers have not attempted to add new and different knowledge to the profession. Instead, the emphasis has intentionally been on making the concepts of information science readable to practitioners. Many adept in information science may find sections that lack the mathematical

1. C. P. Snow, *The Two Cultures: and a Second Look* (Cambridge: Cambridge University Press, 1964), p. 3.

precision that is the common language of the discipline. To a small extent statistical nuance has been sacrificed for comprehension.

A basic premise of this book is that information science and library science are not two separate entities that are slowly moving away from each other; rather, each discipline is part of the same fundamental continuum. Martha Hale has provided the idea that the information profession can be classed along a "theory-practice" continuum:[2]

Theory-Theory	Theory-Practice	Practice-Practice
—— | ————————	| ————————	| ——

The "theory-practice" continuum has suggested the organizational framework for this volume. The book has three parts: Part 1 will provide a general overview of the theory of information science and will set the stage for the chapters that follow; Part 2 will examine some of the key concepts of information science from a theory-practice point of view by reviewing the fundamental ideas in the field of the arrangement and retrieval of information; and Part 3 will demonstrate how information can be applied in the practical environment of library organizations in order to increase their effectiveness. A synopsis of the components of each part follows.

Part 1: Information Science Theory

Chapter 1 gives the reader a broad view of information science theory. It defines information science in terms of its goals and purposes, and attempts to portray the future direction of research.

Chapter 2 deals with the subject of quantitatively describing groups of information sources. Danny P. Wallace investigates the field of bibliometrics and its utilization in modifying information systems.

Chapter 3 explores the relatively new application of linguistic concepts to information system design. Chingkwei Lee and John Olsgaard survey the manner in which the use of language can affect information flow.

Part 2: The Arrangement and Retrieval of Information

Chapter 4 presents an introduction to the foundations of information storage and retrieval. Susan Bonzi examines the manner in which information is manipulated through the use of indexing, vocabulary control, and thesaurus design.

Chapter 5 exposes the reader to the basic concepts of database design and management. Carol Tenopir demonstrates how current computer-based database systems are formulated and fashioned.

2. Martha Hale, presentation made at the Annual Conference of the American Library Association, San Francisco, 27 June 1987.

Chapter 6 presents an explanation of how database searching techniques can affect local practice and utilization. Christyn Billinsky demonstrates how common search categories work and interact with computer-based database designs.

Part 3: The Practice of Information Science in Library Organizations

Chapter 7 examines the effect of information system design on the overall effectiveness of organizations. Michael G. Bowen and Patricia Bick determine how information science concepts can affect the policy-making decisions within organizations.

Chapter 8 describes the formation and administration of automating information systems in libraries. John E. Evans presents an overview of the factors that influence the design of local systems in libraries.

Chapter 9 addresses the problem of determining the adequacy of information systems. F. W. Lancaster examines the concepts of measuring the flow of information and evaluating the adequacy of particular systems.

PART

1

Information Science Theory

CHAPTER

1

A Brief Overview of Information Science Theory

John N. Olsgaard

This chapter starts with one of those "Did you hear the one about the . . ." stories: Did you hear the one about the pollster who came upon two men fishing? The pollster asked both of them to consider what was the greatest invention ever created. The first fisherman said, "The computer, because it's got all those little electrical doodads in it. You can put all kinds of stuff in it, and it will give you back all kinds of things." The pollster dutifully wrote this down and then asked the second fisherman the same question. The second fisherman replied, "The Thermos bottle." The pollster wanted to know why the Thermos bottle was so great. The fisherman said, "Well, when you put hot stuff in it, it stays hot; and when you put cold stuff in it, it stays cold." The pollster said, "There is nothing so great about that." To which the fisherman said, "Yes, but how does it know which is which?"

We know that the process of human cognition allows us to transfer ideas to others in the form of written or spoken symbols that become reassembled ideas in the mind of the receiver. Like the fisherman, our question in much of information theory is "Yes, but how does it know?" How does the mind make this transference from symbols to thought? Is there a recognizable pattern to this transference, and if there is a pattern, how can it be optimized? Information science tries to answer these questions, and to discern "how it knows."

The primary purpose of this chapter is to describe, at a general level, the research focus of each of the major subdisciplines of information science. The secondary purpose is to give a brief description of where some of the elements in the field of information science fit together and overlap. Additionally, an effort is made to identify some of the early leaders of the discipline and to explore some of the more basic terms that are expanded on later in the book.

Perhaps the most difficult thing that you can ask an information scientist is to define information science. Many will say that it can't be defined because information science is an "evolving" science, which is a clever academic way of saying that we really aren't sure. Others will say that information science is simply whatever information scientists happen to be studying. As one might guess from this answer, there are no clear boundaries that make up the field.

3

Information science is a hybrid of many fields of inquiry. This interdisciplinary approach has led to some interesting changes in the faculty makeup of many schools of library and information science. For example, alongside the professor whose specialty is the traditional area of library services will be a specialist in the sociology of knowledge or a specialist in communication theory.

For purposes of this chapter and as a working definition, information science is considered to be the study of the formation, organization, storage, retrieval, and transmission of information. Although this may be more of a listing than a definition, it may serve to illustrate some of the more common areas of study in information science.

Formation of Information

The broadest based and most philosophical area of the various information science branches is the formation of information. This area asks the question "How do people think?" This question of how knowledge is formed is substantial because if this concept were understood it would be theoretically possible to replicate the process in machines. This branch of applied information science is called artificial intelligence (AI). The goal of artificial intelligence research is to create a computer model that will allow the machine to really "think"; that is, to not only follow repetitive instructions but to reach independent conclusions.

A popular form of artificial intelligence is referred to as "expert systems." Expert systems are computer programs which allow machine decision making on a very narrow basis in a limited field of expertise. For instance, some stock trading expert systems allow the computer, under the proper circumstances, to execute trading actions. At best, expert systems are seen as an intermediary step toward the ideal of true artificial intelligence.

Human Thinking—Computer Processing

It is important to understand that much of the early development of computers as a genre was to mimic what was believed to be the way that the human brain works. Individuals are constantly processing information; that is, we are always thinking about something. In fact, humans have the ability to think about several different things at the same time. For instance, the human brain monitors vital functions (e.g., circulation, breathing, digestion) without the individual having to actively think about them. At the same time the individual can be driving a car or writing poetry. What is truly amazing is that the brain can process these different things, using huge amounts of information, and do it all at incredible speed.

In the analogous area of computer development the emphasis has been on: (1) the amount of processing, and (2) the speed of processing. The amount of processing has closely followed the evolution of microchip technology. The early microcomputers used a 16K microchip as a processor, meaning that it could process 16 thousand bits of information at one time. Currently, many computers use a 256K chip, and soon the industry will see the introduction of megachips, or chips that can handle 1 million bits of information at the same time. For microcomputers the amount of processing ability is usually expressed as random access memory (RAM). Large computers, sometimes referred to as mainframes, have central processing units (CPUs), whose capabilities are measured in terms of millions of instructions per second.

The speed of processing issue in the development of computers has focused on two areas: parallel processing and superconductivity. Parallel processing is the effort to allow computers to work on different tasks at the same time. Superconductivity is the area of computer engineering that is trying to get circuitry to work with zero physical resistance, thereby allowing computer operations to be conducted at very fast speeds. The object of these areas of research is to allow computers to process large amounts of information, on several different levels, very quickly—in short, to imitate the human process of thinking.

Short-Term Memory

While the human brain is actively thinking about driving a car or writing poetry, it has nearly instantaneous access to information in short-term memory. This memory includes information that we use on a frequent basis. For example, we can reply quickly to the questions "What is your name?" and "Where do you work?" Short-term memory can also be seen as the place the brain keeps information that is retained for only a short time. For instance, when we look up a phone number in the directory, we usually retain that information only as long as it takes to dial the phone. The conclusion was reached that there must be a place in the brain, or a process, to put information that we utilize all the time or will need only a short time. In terms of computer development, devices of limited storage capability were sought that would allow quick access to information. In microcomputers this device is usually a floppy disk; in large computers the device is called a disk-pack (which looks a little like a cake carrier with record albums stacked inside). These devices allow a computer to store and retrieve limited amounts of information very quickly.

Long-Term Memory

When people are asked what their names are, they can respond from short-term memory reasonably fast. The brain uses a different process to answer something that it normally doesn't think about very often. For instance, if someone should ask, "What was the name of your fourth grade teacher?" most people would have to stop and think about the question for awhile before they could respond. The conclusion that was reached is that the brain uses a different process for storing information that isn't used very often. That is, it would appear that most people have to concentrate harder and take longer to retrieve information of this variety.

In terms of computers, devices were sought that would allow large storage of information that isn't needed very often. Speed of access was traded off for capacity. For microcomputers this technology has meant the advent of hard-disk drives and compact disk–read only memory (CD-ROM). Large computers normally use magnetic tape for long-term storage.

In the attempt to determine the technological mechanisms for emulating human thought, many diverse disciplines have come into play. Computer scientists and computer engineers have tried to design machines with the characteristics of human thought patterns. Cognitive psychologists and those involved in neurophysics have sought to discover exactly what physically happens in the brain when individuals think. Philosophers have examined what constitutes the act of thinking. All have an essential part in the continuing process of putting together a computer that can in some way emulate nature.

Organization and Storage for Retrieval of Information

To librarians and information specialists, organization and storage for retrieval of information may be the most familiar area of information science. For instance, on the most basic level, the Dewey Decimal system is simply a device for providing an overall framework for placing information in a scheme that will allow an individual to find or retrieve a given piece of information once it has been stored. On a more theoretical level, the information scientist asks, "What does the organization of information in a given discipline demonstrate about the discipline itself?"

The relative organization of a given discipline can reveal a great deal about how the discipline is developing. One subdiscipline involved in the examination of the growth of information is bibliometrics. Bibliometrics can be described as a family of statistical distributions which helps describe the growth of knowledge. For instance, bibliometrics can help information agencies to identify which materials and authors are central to a given discipline's growth.

Two of the founding fathers of bibliometrics and citation analysis are: Derek de Solla Price, whose work *Little Science, Big Science* is still considered somewhat of a classic in the field; and Eugene Garfield, whose *Science Citation Index* and subsequent works brought the area of citation analysis into full flower.[1] In the field of information storage and retrieval there were several important early researchers, including Mortimer Taube, F. W. Lancaster, Joseph Becker, and Robert Hayes.

As the name implies, the storage and retrieval of information are concerned with compiling information in one setting and effectively getting it back again. The storage and retrieval of information have become increasingly important to librarians in recent years because of the growth of the number and use of online databases. The two most relevant factors in the study of storage and retrieval of information are speed and accuracy. During the history of online services these

---

1. It is always hazardous to name major contributors to any field because of the problem of leaving out the names of others of equal importance. The materials cited at the end of this chapter and of the chapters that follow give a much more complete listing of those whose work has led to the formation of information science.

two factors have been nearly exclusive. That is, to increase the speed of access one had to decrease the accuracy of the information retrieved. For example, in order to increase the speed of searching, librarians tend to index items according to a finite list of access points (e.g., the Library of Congress List of Subject Headings). A compendium of these access points is collectively known as a "thesaurus." The smaller the list of access points the faster one can search through them. Unfortunately, as the list of access points gets smaller the ability of the system to differentiate between similar but different items decreases.

The advent of the speed of operation of computer-assisted databases allowed a gradual convergence of the speed versus accuracy equation. With the use of computers the number of access points could be greatly increased without substantially decreasing the speed of the system. The logical end product of this reasoning was to create an access point for every conceivable point of retrieval. The forerunner of this type of indexing was Hans Peter Luhn. Luhn created various types of keyword indexing structures, sometimes referred to as KWIC or KWOC indexes, that allowed a computer to index a document by every significant word in its title or text. Various editions of keyword indexes also allowed for the addition of synonym structures.

If anything, the problem with early keyword indexing was that it went too far in the other direction: instead of too few access points, the searcher was faced with the retrieval of too much information. Although the use of Boolean operators (i.e., using the logical form of "and," "or," and "not" as search delimiters) has helped, a good deal of the current information science research in this area involves the search for the correct balance between access and accuracy on one hand and speed of the system on the other. One alternative has been to extensively explore the possibility of increasing accuracy through the use of "string indexing" or "neighbor" programs. That is, the meaning of a term is refined by the specific use of the words surrounding it.

Transmission and Use of Information

The transmission and use of the information branch of information science seeks answers to the question "When we read or hear information, what process do we go through to translate this information into usable knowledge?" The primary disciplines involved in this research include linguistics, communications, and computer science. The basic assumption of this line of inquiry is that information transmission involves the sender of the information formulating a set of symbols representing the idea that he or she wishes to send; transmitting those symbols; and the receiver of the transmission translating those symbols back into an idea. The purpose of information science in this field is to study and understand the complex pattern of symbols that is used for this transmission.

A number of analogies of this process are possible. One example is to compare this process to listening to a radio. At one end of the process an announcer speaks into a microphone. The announcer's speech is translated into a precise set of energy patterns that makes up radio waves sent through the atmosphere. The radio receiving set in an individual's house captures the radio waves and translates the pattern back into human speech. To the information scientist, language in both its written and spoken forms represents the radio waves sent between individuals. It is known that the process of sending and receiving knowledge works; what is not known is exactly how it works.

The focus of much of the research in this subdiscipline has been on a logical basis for the manner in which language is used. When we see or hear words, what process in the brain translates them into images, ideas, and information? A primary obstacle faced in this endeavor is that, like background noise on a radio, people tend to introduce unexplained variants into language; that is, we introduce new words into the language, or we use slang. The problem is that by using illogical variants in the transmission of information we often confuse the meaning that we sought to highlight.

One of the objectives of this subdiscipline has been to take the patterns that are recognizable in language and program a computer to translate material according to meaning and content. This effort is often referred to as natural language processing (NLP). The immediate focus of NLP is to program a computer to successfully index and organize fulltext material that it is given. In effect, the computer would take a given fulltext document and, by comparing it to a set of predetermined linguistic standards, be able to determine the meaning of that material. The end result of this research is to allow normal conversation between man and machine without use of an intermediary command structure. In other words, an individual could talk to a computer and it would understand and talk back.

Summary

One of the reasons that a theory of information science is so difficult to pin down is that it brings together, in several forms, many different intellectual disciplines. Information science, in its pure form, attempts to determine how we think, store, retrieve, and transmit information. Researchers have tried to answer these questions by quantitatively describing what goes on in life, or *in vivo*. The *in vitro*, or what happens in an artificial environment, branch of information science occurs when information scientists attempt to apply what has been discovered about humans to the machine environment. Although computers certainly play an important part in the process of information science applications, computers are only the mechanism by which the theory of information science is implemented.

The aim of information science is to further what we know and can utilize from the flow of information. The objective of both the *in vivo* and *in vitro* forms of information science is to dramatically improve our knowledge of the human condition, and through its applications, to improve the environment in which we live and work. This process of "knowing" has just begun.

Further Reading

American Society for Information Science. *Journal of the American Society for Information Science* 35:147–169 (May 1984); 35:277–319 (September 1984).

Hellprin, Laurence B., ed. *Towards Foundations of Information Science.* White Plains, N.Y.: Knowledge Industry Publications, 1985.

Machlup, Fritz and Una Mansfield, eds. *The Study of Information: Interdisciplinary Messages.* New York: John Wiley & Sons, 1983.

CHAPTER

2

Bibliometrics and Citation Analysis

Danny P. Wallace

Bibliometrics is the application of quantitative methods to the study of information resources. Although work that is now recognized as being bibliometric in nature was conducted more than seventy years ago, the term itself dates only from 1969, when it was proposed by Alan Pritchard as a replacement for the earlier term "statistical bibliography."[1] Two other areas of study that are very closely related to bibliometrics are scientometrics, which encompasses all quantitative analyses of scientific productivity, and citation analysis, which refers to the practices and patterns of scholarly references.

The major focus of bibliometrics is the search for regular patterns related to the characteristics of information sources. Some of the questions asked by bibliometric studies are:

In what countries is the literature of a particular subject or discipline published, and what is the balance of the contributions of those nations?

In what countries do the authors who contribute to a particular subject literature work, and what is the balance of the contributions of those nations?

What languages are most used in publications on a particular subject?

How are words used in publications, and what patterns describe their use?

What types of information sources (books, articles, theses, etc.) are most important to a particular subject?

What research methodologies (historical, case study, experimental, survey, etc.) are most used in a particular subject's research information sources?

What types of articles (research report, opinion piece, news story, etc.) make up the periodical literature of a subject?

What patterns pertain to age of information sources at the time they are used?

What is the distribution of authors' contributions to a literature, and why do some authors publish more than others?

The author wishes to thank Joan Giglierano for her assistance in the preparation of this chapter.

1. Alan Pritchard, "Statistical Bibliography or Bibliometrics?" *Journal of Documentation* 25:348–349 (December 1969).

10

What is the distribution of articles on a particular subject among the journals in which they are published?

What patterns apply to the circulation of items within libraries or their use within libraries?

How can knowledge of bibliometric processes contribute to the operations of libraries and other information systems?

The Origins of Bibliometrics

There were a few efforts in the late nineteenth century that might be considered protobibliometric studies, but the first work that can truly be considered bibliometric in nature was that of Cole and Eales in 1917.[2] In this work, the authors provided a detailed analysis of three centuries of publications in comparative anatomy, emphasizing the growth of the literature and the relative contributions of the European countries. A landmark early work was E. Wyndham Hulme's 1923 study of the *International Catalogue of Scientific Literature*; it was in this work that the term "statistical bibliography" was first used.[3] Hulme addressed a number of bibliometric characteristics of the publications listed in the *Catalogue*, including the sizes of the literatures of different sciences, the number of journals in each science, and the number of journals produced by each country represented in the list. Most of the bibliometric studies carried out during the first half of the twentieth century were independent efforts by scholars in diverse fields who were apparently unaware of one another's works. Since the late 1940s, bibliometrics has flourished, becoming a major subdiscipline within information science.

Lotka's Law: Author Productivity

In 1926, Alfred J. Lotka examined author productivity and proposed the mathematical pattern that has since become known as Lotka's Law.[4] The basis for Lotka's Law, like that of most bibliometric principles, is straightforward and intuitive: for any body of literature, there will be a substantial number of authors who have each contributed only one publication, a smaller number of authors who have each contributed a small number of publications, and a very small group of authors who have each contributed a substantial number of publications. Based on a study of the literatures of physics and chemistry, Lotka concluded that the number of authors making a given number of contributions (n contributions) to a specific body of literature is about $1/n^2$ of the number of authors

2. F. J. Cole and Nellie B. Eales, "The History of Comparative Anatomy. Part I. A Statistical Analysis of the Literature," *Science Progress* 11:578–596 (1917).

3. E. Wyndham Hulme, *Statistical Bibliography in Relation to the Growth of Modern Civilization* (London: Grafton and Company, 1923).

4. Alfred J. Lotka, "The Frequency Distribution of Scientific Productivity," *Journal of the Washington Academy of Sciences* 16:323 (1926).

making one contribution. He further suggested that authors making only one contribution will typically account for about 60 percent of the total number of publications. If, for instance, a body of 1,000 publications is considered, about 600 authors will have each contributed one article. The number of authors who have each contributed two publications will be approximately one-fourth of the number contributing one publication each, or about 150. The number of authors who have each made three contributions will be about one-ninth of the number who have contributed one publication each, or about 67. The number of authors who have made ten contributions each will be about one one-hundredth of 600, or 6. In practice, Lotka's Law tends to break down at the upper end of productivity: most bodies of literature include a very small number of authors who are much more productive than the Law would indicate.

Zipf's Law: The Distribution of Words in Text

Another intuitive principle that has become part of the research base of bibliometrics is the tendency for people to use only a small part of their available vocabulary for most communication. The frequency with which words are represented in text was extensively studied by George K. Zipf. Zipf's work was first presented in 1933,[5] and was later expanded upon in his *Human Behavior and the Principle of Least Effort*.[6] Zipf introduced the concept of "word-types" and "word-tokens." Word-types are distinct words used in a body of text; a listing of all word-types in the text would constitute the complete vocabulary of the text. Word-tokens are distinct occurrences of word-types. When word-tokens are counted, it is possible to generate a ranked list of the frequency with which each word-type occurs in the text. According to Zipf's Law, if r is the rank order of the frequency of occurrence of a given word-type, and f is the actual frequency of occurrence, then $r * f = c$, where c is some constant number unique to the body of literature being studied. C has usually been found to be approximately equal to one-tenth of the total number of word-tokens in the body of text being studied. For instance, comparing the three words "library," "circulation," and "acquisitions" in a hypothetical text might produce the following results:

Word	Frequency (f)	Rank (r)	r*f=c
Library	66	1	66
Circulation	22	3	66
Acquisitions	33	2	66

A graph of the relationship between word-type frequency and word-type rank produces the very distinctive curve shown in Figure 2.1. For most bodies of text, the formula provided by Zipf is quite accurate for the middle range of frequen-

5. George K. Zipf, *The Psycho-Biology of Language* (Boston: Houghton Mifflin Company, 1935).

6. George K. Zipf, *Human Behavior and the Principle of Least Effort* (Cambridge, Mass.: Addison-Wesley Press, 1949).

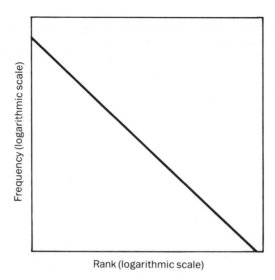

Rank (logarithmic scale)

Figure 2.1. The Zipf rank-frequency distribution

cies, but not for very frequent or very infrequent words. At one extreme of the distribution there are typically a few words, such as conjunctions, prepositions, and articles, that occur with a greater frequency than that allowed for by the formula. At the other extreme there are usually a few rare and sometimes esoteric words that occur much less frequently than the formula would suggest. The general pattern, however, has been found to hold for a substantial variety of bodies of text, and its regularity is rather amazing.

Bradford's Law: The Scatter of Literature

The bibliometric principle that has probably received the most attention is scatter. Scatter (also called dispersion or productivity) is based on the frequently observed fact that the use of any collection of items is rarely distributed evenly: some items are heavily used, others receive moderate use, and some are used rarely or not at all. It has been found that the distribution patterns of the use of such items are quite regular and predictable. Measures of scatter include "yearly circulation or other use of a book or journal, number of articles on a given field in the given journal," and "number of references to the given article in subsequent journals."[7]

The most prominent model for scatter is Bradford's Law. In 1934, Samuel C. Bradford examined the literatures of applied geophysics and lubrication and observed a marked regularity in the distribution of articles in relationship to the

---

7. Philip M. Morse and Ferdinand F. Leimkuhler, "Exact Solution for the Bradford Distribution and Its Use in Modeling Informational Data," *Operations Research* 27:187 (January–February 1979).

journals in which they had been published.[8] Bradford suggested that for each of the two bibliographies studied it was possible to divide the articles into three zones, each of which included an approximately equal number of articles, while the number of journals required to produce those articles increased substantially and regularly from one zone to the next. Bradford formulated a "law of scattering" to characterize this regularity:

> If scientific journals are arranged in order of descending productivity of articles on a given subject, they may be divided into a nucleus of periodicals more particularly devoted to the subject and several groups or zones containing the same number of articles as the nucleus, when the number of periodicals in the nucleus and succeeding zones will be as $1:n:n^2$.[9]

The bibliography of applied geophysics used by Bradford, for instance, conformed to the following pattern:

Zone	Number of Journals	Number of Articles
1	9	429
2	59	499
3	258	404

The starting point for a Bradford analysis is preparation of a ranked list of journals, beginning with the journal that produced the most articles and ending with those journals that each produced one article. This list is then turned into two columns of related figures: the first column provides a cumulative listing of the number of journals, while the second provides a cumulative listing of the number of articles contributed by that number of journals.

When the numbers of journals and of articles are cumulated and plotted on a semilogarithmic graph, the very distinctive curve of Figure 2.2 is produced. The curve consists of three major areas: a long straight section that represents the major portion of the bibliography, a lower curved section that has been called the "Bradford restriction," and an upper curved portion sometimes referred to as the "Groos droop." A number of authors have developed sophisticated formulae for characterizing the shape of the curve and determining the extent to which a particular bibliography is truly Bradfordian, and a large portion of the literature of Bradford's Law has to do with the comparison, refinement, and testing of these formulae.

Bradford's Law has been found to hold for the distribution of articles among journals in most literatures, although the specific shape of the curve varies according to the size and nature of the bibliography. Although most tests of the Bradford distribution have utilized subject bibliographies, Bradford's Law has sometimes been applied to more general collections, including

---

8. S. C. Bradford, "Sources of Information on Specific Subjects," *Engineering* 137:85–86 (1934).

9. Ibid., 86.

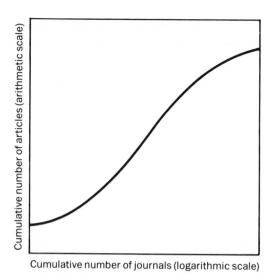

Figure 2.2. The Bradford distribution

those of a special library[10] and a liberal arts college.[11] Bradford's law has also been successfully applied to the study of monograph publishers,[12] library circulation,[13] "the scatter among periodicals of references actually read by a group of scientists,"[14] the distribution of reference questions per requester,[15] the distribution of users of journals in a circulating collection,[16] and the distribution of photocopy requests.[17]

Garfield has suggested that there is actually a Bradford distribution that applies to *all* scientific journals, and has referred to this as a "law of concentration."[18] Holdings of the British Library suggest that the number of

10. E. F. Hockings, "Selection of Scientific Periodicals in an Industrial Research Library," *Journal of the American Society for Information Science* 25:132 (March–April 1974).

11. Martin Gordon, "Periodicals Use at a Small College Library," *Serials Librarian* 6:63–73 (Summer 1982).

12. James C. Baughman, "Toward a Structural Approach to Collection Development," *College and Research Libraries* 38:241–248 (May 1977); Dennis B. Worthen, "The Application of Bradford's Law to Monographs," *Journal of Documentation* 31:19–25 (March 1975).

13. Stephen Bulick, "Book Use as a Bradford-Zipf Phenomenon," *College and Research Libraries* 39:218 (May 1978); Allen Kent and others, *Use of Library Materials: The University of Pittsburgh Study* (New York: M. Dekker, 1977), 38.

14. B. C. Vickery, "Bradford's Law of Scattering," *Journal of Documentation* 4:198 (December 1948).

15. P. F. Cole, "The Analysis of Reference Question Records as a Guide to the Information Requirements of Scientists," *Journal of Documentation* 14:197– 207 (December 1958).

16. Paul B. Mayes, "The Use of the Bradford-Zipf Distribution to Estimate Efficiency Values for a Journal Circulation System," *Journal of Documentation* 31:287–289 (December 1975).

17. Donald J. Morton, "Analysis of Interlibrary Requests by Hospital Libraries for Photocopied Journal Articles," *Bulletin of the Medical Library Association* 65:425–432 (October 1977).

18. Eugene Garfield, "Citation Analysis as a Tool in Journal Evaluation," *Science* 178:476 (October 27, 1972).

scientific journals published worldwide is something like 50,000. According to Garfield's Law of Concentration, this number can be divided into three zones as follows:

Zone	Number of Journals
1	1,000
2	6,500
3	42,500

The first zone is presumably made up of multidisciplinary journals and journals that constitute the core of research in specific subject areas. The second zone includes journals that are of a more specialized nature and therefore do not have the broad significance of the first zone journals, and the third zone consists of journals that are of a very highly specialized nature, are of purely local interest, or for some other reason do not contribute as strongly to the overall body of scientific literature.

Obsolescence: The Decline in Use of Materials as They Age

Most experienced librarians are well aware that items in their collection tend to attract less use the older they get. In many libraries this factor is used as a rationale for discarding older items, and the process of determining the point at which an item has become so old that it should be discarded is an important collection management issue. This aging process has also been observed in the context of the references included in scholarly publications: most references tend to be to relatively recent publications, and the likelihood of a publication being cited appears to decline over time. This aging process is generally referred to as "obsolescence," although the aging of information sources and the obsolescence of a technology or methodology clearly are not directly analogous. When a piece of machinery is said to be obsolescent, there is usually the implication that it has been replaced by a better piece of machinery and is therefore no longer of use. Obsolescence in bibliometrics, however, suggests only that older materials are not used, not that they are no longer useful.

Obsolescence has usually been studied in the context of the circulation of items in a library collection, or of the citation of one body of literature by another. The results of obsolescence studies are quite consistent: when items are ranked according to their age at the time they are used (circulated, requested, cited, etc.), recent items account for a very large proportion of the items used, while very old items receive very little use. This distribution tends to conform to the pattern shown in Figure 2.3. Obsolescence is sometimes described in terms of the "half-life" of a literature. The basic definition of the half-life of a literature is "the time during which one-half of all the currently active literature was published."[19] Although most studies of obsolescence have addressed aging

---

19. R. E. Burton and R. W. Kebler, "The 'Half-Life' of Some Scientific and Technical Literatures," *American Documentation* 11:18–19 (January 1960).

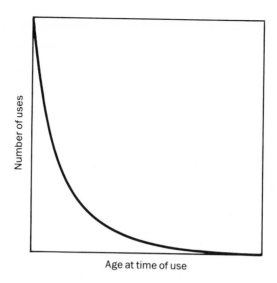

Figure 2.3. The obsolescence curve

qualities of entire literatures, it has been suggested that "what librarians need to know is how long they need to keep individual journals. For this, *item half-life* figures for each of the journals are ideally required."[20]

Obsolescence studies have been conducted of diverse materials in a variety of environments, including periodical use in a small biomedical library,[21] book circulation in a major medical library,[22] the date distribution of periodicals circulated in a large public library,[23] the circulation of books in a university library,[24] the use of physics[25] and biomedical[26] journals in academic libraries, and photocopy requests in a pharmaceutical library.[27] Although the shape of the curve is dependent upon the specific circumstances of the study, the general nature of the obsolescence curve shown in Figure 2.3 appears to be universal.

20. M. B. Line, "The 'Half-Life' of Periodical Literature: Apparent and Real Obsolescence," *Journal of Documentation* 26:47 (March 1970).

21. Judith Wallen Hunt, "Periodicals for the Small Bio-Medical and Clinical Library," *Library Quarterly* 7:121–140 (January 1937).

22. Frederick G. Kilgour, "Recorded Use of Books in the Yale Medical Library," *American Documentation* 12:266–269 (October 1961).

23. Peter Spyers-Duran, "The Use of Periodicals in a Large Public Library," *Wilson Library Bulletin* 36:299–300 (December 1961).

24. Kent and others, 16–18.

25. Ching-Chih Chen, "The Use Patterns of Physics Journals in a Large Academic Research Library," *Journal of the American Society for Information Science* 23:254–265 (July–August 1972).

26. Michael V. Sullivan and others, "Obsolescence in Biomedical Journals: Not an Artifact of Literature Growth," *Library Research* 2:29–45 (Spring 1980–81).

27. Victor A. Basile and Reginald W. Smith, "Evolving the 90% Pharmaceutical Library," *Special Libraries* 61:81–86 (February 1970).

Citation Studies: The Paper Trail in Scholarly Publication

The practice of giving credit to the sources of information used by an author in preparing a publication has a long history and is considered an integral and fundamental part of scholarly activity. Because it is such a basic activity, it has also become the subject of considerable study. The first citation study was probably that of Gross and Gross in 1927, in which the authors explored the use of citation counts as a selection tool for journals in chemistry.[28] Some of the questions addressed by citation studies are:

What motivates an author to cite a particular work?

What is the relationship between a citing work and the works cited by it?

Why are some works cited long after their publication while others are cited only when relatively new?

Why are some works heavily cited while others are cited infrequently or not at all?

How do citation practices and patterns differ among disciplines or families of disciplines?

How can citation practices and patterns be used in the evaluation of information sources?

How can citation practices and patterns be used to enhance information retrieval systems?

The fundamental assumptions of most citation studies include:

The citing author has actually used the cited work and has cited all works used.

Citation of an information source is an indicator of its quality.

The citing author has provided references to the best possible works.

Content of the citing work is significantly related to the content of the cited works.

All citations are of equal value.

Smith has provided a good summary of the rationales for and problems of these assumptions as part of an overview of the nature and use of citation analysis.[29] The overall conclusion that can be drawn is that none of the assumptions is universally true, although each may be true under certain circumstances.

One major problem of citation analysis is that many factors can motivate an author to cite another work, and determining the true relationship between citing and cited publications may require an understanding of the specific motives for a given act of citation. These factors can include a desire to give the appearance of being in touch with the most recent literature, the need to provide support for a methodology or tool, attempts to persuade the reader of the correctness and importance of the ideas being presented, providing appropriate credit for the

28. P. L. K. Gross and E. M. Gross, "College Libraries and Chemical Education," *Science* 66:385–389 (October 28, 1927).

29. Linda C. Smith, "Citation Analysis," *Library Trends* 30:83–106 (Summer 1981).

origin of ideas, alerting the reader to important publications, establishing evidence of a consensus of opinion among researchers, and refutation of the claims of other researchers. Brooks found that the balance among these factors is quite variable and that motivations may represent a complex combination of factors.[30] Other research has suggested that the point within a publication at which a reference is given cannot be successfully used as an indicator of the motivation for citation.[31] Despite these limitations, the notion that citation represents a rather constant indication of the relationship between one information source and another lies at the heart of most citation studies, and plays a key role in the practical application of citation analysis.

Citation analysis has also been extensively explored as a means for evaluating the work of institutions and individuals. The data provided by *Science Citation Index*, *Social Sciences Citation Index*, and *Arts & Humanities Citation Index*, particularly in their online forms, can readily be exploited for

> obtaining lists of publications by a given author, for determining centers of certain types of research, for comparative evaluations of academic departments, and for evaluation of peers in tenure and promotion considerations.[32]

These applications of citation analysis have been the subject of considerable controversy and have been regarded with a mixture of acceptance, trepidation, and scorn. A listing of publications obtained from such a source may not represent all of an author's output, and the assumption that it does may result in a faulty assessment of the author's contribution to his or her field. Similarly, citation counts will represent only citations from the journals covered by the citation index and cannot honestly be assumed to represent all possible citations to an author's work. There is also a substantial potential for error in determining whether citations should really be attributed to a given author, since the citation indexes provide only the author's last name and initials and are subject to virtually no authority control. The uneducated use of citation counts for evaluative purposes of any kind can have disastrous results, and a very real problem of citation analysis is application of results by individuals who are not capable of effectively interpreting them.

The Theoretical Basis of Bibliometrics and Citation Analysis

Bibliometrics and citation analysis both provide ways of examining the patterns of activity related to information sources. A potential limitation of bibliometrics and citation analysis is the lack of a well-developed unified theoretical base to

---

30. Terrence A. Brooks, "Evidence of Complex Citer Motivations," *Journal of the American Society for Information Science* 37:34–36 (January 1986).

31. Susan Bonzi, "Characteristics of a Literature as Predictors of Relatedness between Cited and Citing Works," *Journal of the American Society for Information Science* 33:208–216 (July 1982).

32. Barbara A. Rice and Tony Stankus, "Publication Quality Indicators for Tenure or Promotion Decisions: What Can the Librarian Ethically Report?" *College and Research Libraries* 44:173 (March 1983).

explain and predict the patterns that have been observed. One proposal that has been presented and explored as an explanation for bibliometric functions is the cumulative advantage theory. This theory, which was developed by Derek de Solla Price, invokes the "Matthew Principle":

> For whosoever has, to him shall more be given, and he shall have an abundance; but whoever does not have, even what he has shall be taken away from him.[33]

In more practical terms, the cumulative advantage theory suggests that all information sources begin with an equal probability of use. Each time an information source is used, however, its likelihood of use increases, while the likelihood of an as-yet-unused information source being used remains constant. By extension, the cumulative advantage theory can be used as a tentative explanation of the "success breeds success" nature of all the bibliometric laws:

> A paper which has been cited many times is more likely to be cited again than one which has been little cited. An author of many papers is more likely to publish again than one who has been less prolific. A journal which has been frequently consulted for some purpose is more likely to be turned to again than one of previously infrequent use. Words become common or remain rare. A millionaire gets extra income faster and easier than a beggar.[34]

The cumulative advantage theory makes it possible to understand that the various bibliometric laws really represent one phenomenon that is closely related to other statistical distributions, including the size distribution for islands described by Mandelbrot and the Pareto Law of Income Distribution. Price's theory has been criticized by others, but the criticisms have generally taken the form of quibbles regarding the exact formulation of equations related to the theory rather than rejections of the theory itself. Although the complete ramifications of the cumulative advantage theory as an explanation of bibliometric phenomena have not yet been revealed, it does serve to provide a preliminary approach to understanding a complex set of related distributions.

Practical Applications of Bibliometrics and Citation Analysis

A common theme of bibliometric studies and citation analyses is that the results of such studies can be of practical assistance in library collection management and the development of new information retrieval systems. The appeal of methods based on bibliometrics lies largely in their emphasis on quantification. Such methods may allow for more scientific approaches to making decisions regarding the selection, retention, and location of bibliographic items in library collections. Similarly, it is possible to apply bibliometric techniques to the process of determining what information sources should be covered by an indexing or abstract-

33. Matthew 13:12 NASB.

34. Derek de Solla Price, "A General Theory of Bibliometric and Other Cumulative Advantage Processes," *Journal of the American Society for Information Science* 27:292 (September–October 1976).

ing service. Citation analysis has been proposed as a means of identifying high-quality publications and has also been used in the development of alternatives to traditional subject indexing.

Some bibliometric principles appear to have no direct applicability to the solution of practical problems. Zipf's Law, for instance, is of interest to linguists and is useful in characterizing the differences among literatures,[35] but has as yet had no direct impact on library practice and has had only a limited effect on the design of information retrieval systems. As fulltext databases become more common, however, Zipf's Law may be applied to the processing of large documents in electronic form, and it has already had some impact on the design of natural language interfaces for information retrieval systems. Similarly, Lotka's Law provides insight into the nature of authorship and can be used in comparing disciplines and their literatures, but it appears to have little potential for explicitly aiding in the design or operation of information systems. The two bibliometric concepts that have been most frequently proposed as potential aids to collection management and information system design are scatter and obsolescence.

Application of the Bradford distribution has frequently been proposed as a means for identifying the journals that are most important to the study of a specific topic, based on the assumption that the most productive journals are also in some way the most valuable. A limitation of this assumption is the lack of sound empirical evidence to support it. Very few studies have been conducted of the relationship between journal productivity and journal quality, and the results of those that have been conducted are mixed. Wallace and Bonzi, in a study of the literature of bibliometrics and citation analysis, found that there was a correlation between journal productivity and the frequency with which journals were cited, but this approach requires acceptance of the unproven assumption that frequency of citation can be used as a measure of quality.[36] Using a different methodology, Lamb found a similar relationship between quality and quantity for the literature of mathematics.[37] Pontigo-Martinez, on the other hand, found no significant relationship between journal productivity and the evaluation of journal articles by a panel of judges,[38] and Boyce and Pollens found no significant correlation between a ranking of mathematics journals by citation and a ranking produced by a Bradford analysis.[39]

Brookes has listed a set of information system design questions that could be answered through proper application of Bradford's Law:

35. Ronald E. Wyllys, "The Measurement of Jargon Standardization in Scientific Writing Using Rank-Frequency ('Zipf') Curves" (Ph.D. dissertation, University of Wisconsin, 1974).

36. Danny P. Wallace and Susan Bonzi, "The Relationship between Journal Productivity and Quality," *Proceedings of the American Society for Information Science* 22:193–196 (1985).

37. Gertrude House Lamb, "The Coincidence of Quality and Quantity in the Literature of Mathematics" (Ph.D. dissertation, Case Western Reserve University, 1971).

38. Jaime Pontigo-Martinez, "Qualitative Attributes and the Bradford Distribution" (Ph.D. dissertation, University of Illinois, 1984).

39. Bert R. Boyce and Janet Sue Pollens, "Citation-Based Impact Measures and the Bradfordian Selection Criteria," *Collection Management* 4:29–36 (Fall 1982).

1. What would be the cost of collecting *all* the journals relevant to a given topic?
2. What fraction of the total coverage would be available at any specified limit of cost?
3. What is the optimum distribution of journal collections between a central reference point and satellite departments or regional collections?
4. How can a given collection best be subdivided into collections of primary, secondary, and tertiary relevance or into stores requiring frequent, occasional, or only rare access?[40]

The model for the use of Bradford's Law that is usually presented involves first conducting a Bradford analysis, then making decisions regarding the level of coverage to be provided as determined by available space, cost of acquiring journals, or some related set of factors. This set of decisions is used to define a cutting point in the distribution to be used in collection management. If, for instance, a fixed amount of money is available for purchasing journals in a specific subject area, it is possible to use a Bradford analysis to identify the most productive journals, and then adopt the strategy of acquiring as many of the most productive journals as the budget will allow. This strategy is particularly appealing in that it will result in the acquisition of those journals that make the greatest number of contributions to the subject literature, and it does not require that explicit decisions be made regarding the relative quality or usefulness of the journals. The strategy is effective even if the subject literature does not conform very well to the Bradford distribution, since

> it is not the zones of productivity, or the exponential nature of the decrease in productivity, but the simple decrease itself that leads to the selection strategy.[41]

The major limiting factor of the strategy is the effort required to gather the data for Bradford analysis. A fairly large body of articles is necessary for an accurate analysis, and it is necessary to conduct the study not just once, but continuously, since journal rankings may change over time. It is conceivable that an automated procedure for evaluating the contents of machine-readable databases could be developed, but no such procedures exist at the present time.

The Bradford distribution also appears to apply to the frequency with which materials are circulated in libraries, and in this area the potential for developing automated procedures is high. As more and more libraries adopt automated circulation systems, it is virtually inevitable that the ability to automatically collect and analyze circulation statistics will become increasingly sophisticated. One augmentation that would require a relatively minimal effort is a procedure for cumulating such statistics in a Bradford manner. Such

40. B. C. Brookes, "The Derivation and Application of the Bradford-Zipf Distribution," *Journal of Documentation* 24:249 (December 1968).

41. Bert R. Boyce and Mark Funk, "Bradford's Law and the Selection of High Quality Papers," *Library Resources & Technical Services* 22:391 (Fall 1978).

an analysis could rather easily be used in making decisions concerning such factors as discarding materials that are infrequently circulated, acquiring additional copies of heavily used materials, and moving materials to remote storage areas.

The principles underlying the study of obsolescence are also of potential use in library collection management:

> If documents are being considered, the interest is probably a practical one in the probability that an item will be required, as a guide to such questions as when to discard older volumes, how long to keep new ones, what sort of retrospective storage and access an information retrieval system should provide, and so on.[42]

The idea that older materials may legitimately be either discarded or relegated to some remote storage area is familiar to all librarians. The problem of employing strategies for discarding or moving to secondary storage lies in determining when an item is old enough to be removed from the primary collection, and decisions are frequently made on the basis of *ad hoc* rules of thumb or vague guesses. Determination of the actual patterns with which use of the collection declines over time can help make it possible to make more informed decisions and reduce the potential for making incorrect decisions. The use of systematic obsolescence studies in collection management, like the use of Bradford analysis studies, is at present hampered by the difficulty of gathering appropriate data.

The simplest application of citation analysis to collection management involves obtaining citation counts for a body of publications and using the counts to rank the sources. If, for instance, the object is to determine the most important journals in a particular subject area, it is possible to (1) identify all the journals that appear to be relevant to the subject; (2) consult the "Journal Citation Reports" section of *Science Citation Index* or *Social Sciences Citation Index* for citation counts; and (3) rank the journals accordingly.

This approach has the appeal of simplicity, but it may produce results that are biased in favor of journals that publish relatively large numbers of articles. This bias can be reduced through the use of "impact factor" rather than gross citation as a measure of importance. An impact factor divides the number of citations to a journal over a fixed period of time by the number of articles available for citation. "Journal Citation Reports" includes impact factors as well as raw citation counts. Similar approaches can be taken to assessing the relative value of monographs or the contributions of different publishers, although gathering data for such studies is at present more difficult than gathering data for ranking journals. Although the relationship between citation and quality remains uncertain, citation is an indicator of use, and a citation-based approach to identifying important information resources does have the potential for producing a listing of the most-used sources.

---

42. Maurice B. Line and A. Sandison, " 'Obsolescence' and Changes in the Use of Literature with Time," *Journal of Documentation* 30:283 (September 1974).

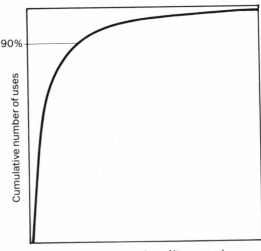

Cumulative number of items used

Figure 2.4. The 90 percent library

The application of bibliometric and citation analysis methods to collection management has sometimes been described in terms of the "90 percent library."[43] The principle of the 90 percent library is based upon the intuitively sound notion that no library can expect to meet all the demands of its users. It may, however, be possible to predict the proportion of needs that can be met, and to plan accordingly. In other words, it is usually not practical to provide service at a *maximum* level, but providing service at some carefully defined *optimum* level may be a reasonable goal. Figure 2.4 provides graphic evidence that there is some point of diminishing returns beyond which major additions of resources are required to achieve minor additional value. The 90 percent figure is arbitrary; the desired performance level for a given library should be based on local needs and requirements.

To a certain extent, the concepts of bibliometrics and citation analysis are ways of systematically looking at situations that are obvious to anyone who has been involved in collection management. Information sources are not all of equal value. In terms of the scatter of a periodical literature, different journals contribute different numbers of articles. In terms of library circulation, some items are heavily used while others are not used at all. In terms of obsolescence, newer items receive more use than older items. In terms of citation, some publications are cited frequently and for a long time, others are cited rarely and only while they are relatively new. The model of the 90 percent library adds a systematic basis to these intuitive conclusions. By graphing the distribution of articles over

43. Charles P. Bourne, "Some User Requirements Stated Quantitatively in Terms of the 90 Percent Library," in Allen Kent and Orrin E. Taulbee, eds., *Electronic Information Handling* (Washington: Spartan Books, 1965), 93–110.

the journals that contribute them in a Bradfordian manner, it is possible to identify those periodicals that should be held in order to achieve some selected percentage of coverage of the literature of a particular field. Similarly, by graphing the distribution of items according to their age at the time they are used, it is possible to determine which items should be held in order to achieve a certain percentage of retrospective coverage. The advantage in conducting such systematic analyses is the removal of guesswork from activities that are fundamental to collection management.

The Future of Bibliometrics and Citation Analysis

Bibliometrics and citation analysis have been the subject of study for three-quarters of a century, but do not appear to have been incorporated into the literature or the practice of collection management. Although collection management journals have included some articles on the use of bibliometrics, they do not seem to have treated bibliometrics as a serious alternative to more traditional methods. Textbooks dealing with the selection, acquisition, and management of publications in libraries generally carry at best a passing reference to bibliometrics and citation analysis. The journals in which bibliometric studies and citation analyses most frequently appear are probably not the journals most frequently read by librarians with collection management responsibilities, and this may contribute to the paucity of published reports on the application of bibliometrics and citation analysis. This does not imply that bibliometrics and citation analysis are not useful as collection management tools, but it does seem to be the case that such methods are not frequently applied to "real world" collection management problems.

The absence of bibliometrics and citation analysis from the toolboxes of collection management librarians may in large part reflect satisfaction with the tools already in use. Quantitative methods require an orientation that is quite different from that necessary for the application of more traditional qualitative methods and require the acquisition of new and different skills. It has also been suggested that "the qualitative methods currently used by librarians allow for a degree of personal control and enjoyment that would not be present if purely quantitative methods were employed."[44] The adoption of new methods inherently involves some element of risk; the limited resources of most libraries and the resultant heavy penalty associated with error may make the risk of exploring new collection management methods intimidating. External forces may in the future provide an increased impetus for the employment of quantitative tools as augmentations to, if not as replacements for, qualitative methods. As Warr has pointed out, "the transition from the affluence of the 1960s to the austerity of the 1980s" has produced a need for more creative collection management practices and a concomitant demand for greater accountability in library budgeting

44. Danny P. Wallace, "A Solution in Search of a Problem: Bibliometrics and Libraries," *Library Journal* 112:47 (May 1, 1987).

and spending.[45] Warr has developed a "favorability index" that adds quantification to the traditional practice of using reviews to judge the quality of publications. This index represents a very positive step in the process of incorporating bibliometrics and citation analysis into the collection management process.

It is possible that the major contributions of bibliometrics and citation analysis lie in areas other than providing direct input into collection management decisions. A major goal of information science is expanding understanding of the ways in which information resources are produced and used, and the ways in which production and use differ among different groups of people. Bibliometrics and citation analysis provide a great deal of potential for accomplishing this goal. The priorities and objectives of a particular set of scholars are surely reflected in their publication activities, and it may therefore be possible to use bibliometric techniques to summarize the character of a discipline and compare it to others. In addition to increasing general understanding of the sociology of scholarly production, bibliometrics and citation analysis may provide a useful indirect contribution to library collection management and other information system functions by replacing poorly formed speculation and traditional wisdom concerning the differences among disciplines with objectively verified data.

At any rate, it is likely that bibliometrics and citation analysis will continue to grow in interest and in scope. There are many problems in both areas that have not yet been adequately addressed. An area that is as yet largely unexplored is the interrelationships among different bibliometric phenomena. Bibliometric principles have not yet been extensively applied to the arts and humanities, or to nonscholarly literatures. The development of programs for incorporating bibliometric procedures into automated systems for libraries and other information systems seems likely. As these and other areas are explored, old questions will be answered and new ones will arise. As answers to new questions are provided, the overall impact and implications of bibliometrics and citation analysis will be better understood.

45. Richard Bruce Warr, "Bibliometrics: A Model for Judging Quality," *Collection Building* 5:29 (Summer 1983).

3

Linguistics and Information Science

Chingkwei Adrienne Lee
and
John N. Olsgaard

The disciplines of linguistics and information science are closely related to each other. Linguistics can be defined as the study of human language as a system for communication, whereas information science is concerned with the communication of information for which language is the primary medium. The study of twentieth-century linguistics has been concerned primarily with oral communication, while information science has focused on written documentation. However, these formalistic delimiters between the two disciplines have increasingly become blurred, and interdisciplinary examinations have recently been started.

The purpose of this chapter is to give a general introduction to linguistics and to examine the manner in which linguistic concepts can be applied to information science.

A Brief Overview of Linguistics

The word "linguistics" was first used in the nineteenth century to emphasize the difference between a newer approach to the study of language that was then developing and the more traditional approach of "philology." The differences were and are largely matters of attitude, emphasis, and purpose. The philologist is concerned primarily with the historical development of languages as it is manifested in written texts and in the context of the associated literature and culture. The linguist tends to give priority to spoken languages and to their structure as they operate at a given point in time, without reference to their history. The linguist, in principle, is interested in all languages and not merely in the great literary languages of the world.

The field of linguistics may be viewed from two different perspectives; the first is in terms of dichotomies, the second is in terms of branches or subdisciplines.

Linguistic Dichotomies

The field of linguistics can be divided into three dichotomies: synchronic versus diachronic, theoretical versus applied, and microlinguistics versus macrolinguistics. A "synchronic" description of a language describes the language as it is at a given time; a "diachronic" description is concerned with the historical development of the language and the structural changes that have taken place in it over successive points in time.

The goal of "theoretical" linguistics is the construction of a general theory of the structure of language or a general theoretical framework for the description of languages. The aim of "applied" linguistics is the application of the findings and techniques of the scientific study of language to a variety of practical tasks, especially to the elaboration of improved methods of language teaching.

"Microlinguistics" refers to a narrower view and "macrolinguistics" to a broader view of the scope of linguistics. According to the microlinguistic view, languages should be analyzed for their own sake and without reference to their social function. Some common areas of interest to the microlinguist would include the manner in which language is acquired by children, the psychological mechanisms that underlie the production and reception of speech, and the literary and the aesthetic or communicative function of language. In contrast, macrolinguistics embraces all of these aspects of language. A number of areas within macrolinguistics have been given terminological recognition: psycholinguistics, sociolinguistics, anthropological linguistics, and stylistics.

Subdisciplines of Linguistics

The second perspective or way of dividing the discipline of linguistics is in terms of branches. The following provides an overview of the branches of linguistics.

Phonetics and Phonology. Both phonetics and phonology deal with language sounds. In phonetics, sound is studied from the point of view of the physiologist (how we make it), the physicist (how the sound waves we produce differ from one another), and the psychologist (how we perceive it). Phonetics generally addresses these areas of interest without much emphasis on the ways in which particular languages use the sounds. For example, one might study the difference between the sound of vowels and consonants in a given language, or between geographic regions using the same language. Phonology, by contrast, stresses how sounds are utilized by languages (e.g., how different languages allow vowels and consonants to be combined with one another in different ways).

Morphology and Syntax. The primary emphasis of morphology and syntax is on words. Morphology concentrates on the internal structures of words—how they are made of smaller parts, such as how the word "dogs" consists of "dog" plus "s." Syntax concentrates on the relationship between words in a sentence; these relationships are often referred to as "constructions." For example, in the sentence "boys like girls," it is morphology that discusses the fact that "s" is added to "boy" and "girl" to make each plural, but it is syntax that allows us to analyze the sentence as consisting of a subject ("boys"), a verb ("like"), and an object ("girls"). Morphology and syntax make up a good deal of what is generally called "grammar."

A common type of morphological analysis utilizes a technique known as "computational linguistics." Generally, computational linguistics is no more than the use of electronic digital computers in linguistic research. At a theoretically trivial level, computers are employed in morphological research to scan texts and to produce, more rapidly and more reliably than was possible in the past, such valuable aids to linguistic and stylistic research as word lists, frequency counts, and concordances. Theoretically more interesting, though much more difficult, is the automatic grammatical analysis of texts by computers.

Semantics and Pragmatics. Semantics and pragmatics examine the meaning of language. The parts of overall meaning that come directly from words and constructions are the province of semantics. The parts of overall meaning that come from the context in which the sentence is uttered are generally handled by pragmatics (sometimes called "applied semantics"). For instance, the meaning of most everyday speech can be conveyed by the cumulative definition of the words used and could be termed semantics. In this way the use of mathematics could be said to have a low level of "syntactic ambiguity"; that is, what is stated in mathematical terms can be interpreted only in a limited number of ways. However, in the case of most humor and poetry, meaning must be transmitted contextually; that is, correct meaning assumes a certain amount of joint cultural knowledge. Thereby, humor could be said to have a high level of syntactic ambiguity.

Although they have been discussed and studied since ancient Greece by scholars and philosophers such as Aristotle, semantics and pragmatics are less highly developed than are other areas of linguistics. Historically, much of the research in semantics has been an attempt to find a quantitative model that will explain how language is used and formulated. In recent years, the focus of research in this branch of linguistics has turned to analysis of "communication in context," rather limiting the scope of linguistic theory to the properties of individual words and sentences. Even in strictly grammatical studies, more and more concentration has been on a functional, communicatively relevant, conception of syntax. In such a perspective, problems like syntactic ambiguity are treated much more than before as the very real problems which they have always been to the common users of language.

Linguistic Concepts in Information Science

The discipline of linguistics increasingly became relevant to the field of information science as linguistics research evolved into examinations of how language is learned and formulated and how language is used to transmit meaning. As pointed out in Chapter 1, fundamental to the long-term quest for achieving a computer with artificial intelligence is an understanding of the human ability for language acquisition and interpretation. In the short term, this understanding could greatly enhance the efficiency of current data retrieval systems.

Language Acquisition

Parents of small children are usually proudly amazed when the children begin not only saying their first words, but soon verbally expressing relatively complex ideas (e.g., trust funds). Linguists have also been intrigued by this phenomenon on a somewhat more objective theoretical level. What mechanism allows humans to learn language, but not most other animals? In the attempt to answer this question, linguists have broken into at least three separate camps.

The "empiricists" have taken the view from psychology that language acquisition is simply the physical response of environmental stimuli (i.e., children talk because everyone around them is talking). As expressed by one of the foremost thinkers of modern linguistics, Noam Chomsky, the "innatists" see language acquisition as an example that humans have some special biological device in their brains (i.e., an innate device) that allows the learning of language. The "constructionists" take somewhat of a middle ground, as proposed by Jean Piaget, between the previous two schools of thought, saying that language is acquired through using general processing skills in conjunction with sensory perception of extant language (i.e., an individual constructs a language ability).[1] The definitive quantitative answering of these proposals will go a long way toward allowing science to replicate this ability in an artificial environment.

Natural Language Processing

With the rapid development of computer technology, it seems clear that most scientists or other professionals of the near future will have an online terminal in their office. They will use this terminal regularly and routinely in the acquisition and dissemination of information. This phenomenon implies: (1) that the design of information services will continue to focus on use of systems by subject specialists rather than by information specialists; (2) that the ability of user-friendly "front-end" devices on computers will continue to be substantially improved; and (3) that the effectiveness and efficiency of computers to process information queries into results will be considerably improved.

The genre of research in information science that is of most interest to linguistics is the field of natural language processing (NLP). In its most general form, NLP simply refers to the ability of the computer to recognize and understand normal language. The concepts of natural language processing can be specified in terms of four subfields: (1) speech recognition; (2) command recognition; (3) content analysis and representation; and (4) system interaction. As illustrated in Figure 3.1, the first two subfields (speech and command recognition) facilitate use by the client. Content analysis and representation are used primarily as an internal function of the computer to correctly translate information to be stored in a database. System interaction is a way of monitoring the effectiveness of the interaction between the client and computer. These components are described as follows.

1. *Speech Recognition.* Use of computers has been tied to the utilization of typewriter keyboards. The essential drawback of keyboards is that while the

1. Ray C. Dougherty, "Current Views of Language and Grammar," in Fritz Machlup and Una Mansfield, eds., *The Study of Information: Interdisciplinary Messages* (New York: John Wiley & Sons, 1983), 321–325.

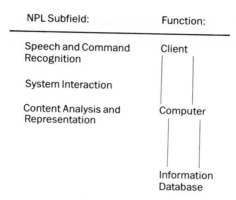

Figure 3.1. Function of NPL subfields in human-machine interaction

speed of the computer may be very fast, the overall speed of transactions has been limited to the rate that an individual can type. For example, this drawback has been a major problem for individuals with physical disabilities who could well profit from automated systems. The obvious answer to the bottleneck created by the keyboard is to eliminate the necessity of inputting data in this manner. One solution is to have the computer recognize voice-activated instructions.

The technological ability of a computer to recognize voice commands and translate those into a digital form is far more complex than one might imagine. Individuals naturally have the ability to process the same words spoken in different accents and recognize the identical meaning. The difficulty is that computers tend to get confused by regional or individual accents (i.e., they "hear" nonunderstandable sounds). A limitation to most current voice recognition systems is that they must be keyed to an individual. In other words, only one person can use a given machine.

The solution is to have a voice recognition system that, like humans, will ignore accent patterns. The study of linguistics has and will make a great contribution in this area. Specifically, if phonetic and phonological studies can identify the variant pronunciations of words in a systematic way, then the computer can be programmed to recognize these variations. If the possible variations of a high percentage of words can be documented, then future voice recognition systems can become generalized.

2. *Command Recognition.* Command recognition is that subfield of NLP that refers to the ability of a computer to properly recognize a command without the user utilizing a formal programming command structure. The object of command recognition systems is for individuals to be able to use a wide variety of computer programs without having to learn a wide variety of computer commands. In current terminology it is common to see references to "user-friendly" systems or "front-end" systems. Both of these terms refer to beginning efforts in com-

mand recognition systems. Front-end systems are discussed in greater detail in Chapter 6. The general schematic of most current user-friendly systems is to take the client through a rather lengthy series of menus.

The focus of future efforts in command recognition systems is to have the client use normal language to use the computer. For example, the client could command the computer, "I need to write a letter." The computer would translate this request to mean load the word processing program and open a new data file in correspondence format. In order for this client request to be understood by the computer, a rather large amount of prior knowledge must be known by system designers in the areas of common syntax (i.e., how people usually use words) and linguistic pragmatics (i.e., what these words mean).

3. *Content Analysis and Representation.* Content analysis of documents is a fundamental property of information storage and retrieval. The roadblock to the complete automation of storage and retrieval databases has been the search for a good way of having the computer system interpret the meaning of the document. Currently, most indexing programs determine meaning with either a morphological approach (i.e., each word in a document is treated separately) or a syntactic approach (i.e., meaning is gained by the use of other words used in the same sentence as the first).

Several formative linguistic projects have recently been initiated to program automated systems to analyze meaning of a document on the basis of the entire text. These projects have used a type of computer program known as a "semantic analyzer." The task for this applied semantics research is to combine traditional syntactic analysis with an analysis of the natural language content of a document semantically and to choose criteria for forming a set of relevant semantic units to be utilized in machine databases. An automated system using a semantic language should be capable of making a decision, on its own, concerning the content of a text and its relevance in relationship to the user's request.

One of the problems of converting the text into a semantic representation is the versatile nature of language. The fact that language can say the same thing in a number of ways requires a very large number of rules to handle natural language texts for even a limited domain. The key to text analysis is organizing this collection of rules. The first thing that must be done is to determine the "structure of information" in the domain whose texts are being processed (i.e., to classify the objects in the domain to form a "semantic class"), and to determine how these objects may combine to form larger structures.

In order to capture the structure of information in a domain, several different formalisms have been developed. Among these is the label "frame-based systems." A frame is a data structure that holds information about an instance of a particular class of objects. Each frame has a set of "slots" which records the properties and components of an object or action; thus a dining room frame may have slots for walls, floor, table, chairs, lights, etc. To capture the information structure of a domain, a network of frames may be assembled and tied together by relationships such as part/whole and generalization/specialization. For exam-

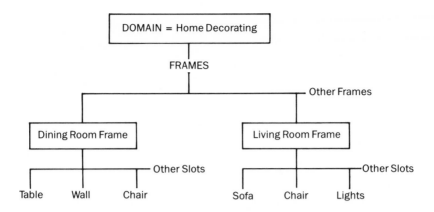

Figure 3.2. Home decorating as an example of frame-based systems

ple, the dining room frame could be considered part of a larger domain, such as "home decorating." Figure 3.2 illustrates these relationships.

Some researchers have developed additional structuring formalisms, using the "conceptual dependency" semantic representation, such as "script." Script involves actors who participate in a series of actions to capture stereotyped sequences of everyday actions. For example, a restaurant script would involve a "patron" and a "waiter": the patron goes to the restaurant, gives the waiter an order, is served by the waiter, eats the meal, receives a bill from the waiter, pays the bill, and leaves the restaurant. Figure 3.3 illustrates the above restaurant script.

Both frames and scripts include constraints and default information which allow a language analyzer to reconstruct implicit information in a narrative. The reason frames and scripts are important is that if linguistic analysis of this nature could be properly utilized in automation, then computers could interpret meaning

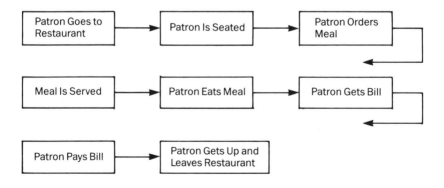

Figure 3.3. Eating in a restaurant as an example of script

by the relationship of a given phrase to a frame or script. Thereby, the effectiveness of expert systems or voice recognition systems would be greatly enhanced.

There are several advantages in using a semantic analyzer for text processing. The advantages are:

a.   A small number of mutually combinable units of minimal semantic nature makes it possible to carry out searching and analytical operations with increased effectiveness.
b.   Semantic equivalents are not solely dependent on the document being analyzed. This quality makes it possible to penetrate "behind the text" and examine the reality modeled by the text.

However, there are also disadvantages in using semantic analysis. The disadvantages include:

a.   Construction of semantic languages is very difficult and requires a large amount of research to formulate.
b.   Expressing the content of specific terms with the help of semantic units is rather complicated and sometimes doubtful. This has been particularly true of attempting to deal with proper nouns.
c.   Translating texts into semantic languages requires a huge amount of computer processing.

For these reasons the ability of automated systems to determine contextual meaning through the large-scale use of linguistic techniques is still in its infancy.

4. *System Interaction.* In much the same fashion that the ideal automated system would relate the client's command to the text of the database, the system would also need to be able to determine if the answers provided were correct. In order to accomplish this, the system must be able to map the client's questions and responses into the relationships used by the database. The relationships constitute the dynamic conceptual model maintained by the system which encompasses the user's queries and the corresponding matchups made with the database. Once the question has been mapped into the relationships used by the database, the system can then refine further questions and translate these again into the particular formalism used by the database system. Again, the use of linguistic techniques would be crucial to the proper functioning of a system like this.

For example, the client could begin, "I need current price information on automobiles." The system would translate this query into the information available in its database and would give its response. The client could then reply, "I'm sorry, I just need this for compact cars." The system should be able to refine the information previously provided to exclude non-needed information (as opposed to the system beginning all over again) and give a focused reply. Figure 3.4 gives an illustration of this interaction.

Client Commands	Computer Internal Response	Computer Response to Client
"Computer, I need current prices on automobiles."	COMMAND: Information Request; DATABASE=Automobiles; SORT="Current Year" INDEX=Price; LIST; RUN;	Cadillac = $XXXXX Audi = $XXXXX Pontiac = $XXXXX • • •
"I need it just for compact cars."	"Cars"=Automobiles; "It"=Price; IF TYPE="Compact" THEN LIST; ELSE DELETE; RUN;	Chev. = $XXXXX Toyota = $XXXXX Nissan = $XXXXX • • •
"But I just wanted ones made in America."	"Ones"=Automobiles; "America"=US; IF COUNTRY=US THEN LIST; ELSE DELETE; RUN;	Chevy = $XXXXX Ford = $XXXXX Dodge = $XXXXX • • •
"Thanks, Computer. That is all for now."	"Thanks, Computer"=NULL; "All for now"=ENDLOOP1; EXECUTE ENDLOOP1; LVOICE="You're welcome"; CLOSE FILES; END RUN; COMMAND:	"You're welcome."

Note: Presumably our computer would also list specific models of cars.

Figure 3.4. Pricing automobiles as an example of system interaction

Conclusion

As is demonstrated in the above discussion, technological advances will not alone be sufficient to bring about large-scale improvements in the quality of individual-machine interaction. The solutions to the problem of preserving meaning lie not only in the findings of computer science and information science but also in the findings of the various branches of linguistics, such as syntax, semantics, and pragmatics. If the goal of artificial intelligence or even the vast improvement in the ease of machine use is to be achieved, it will have to be accomplished with dramatic breakthroughs in the field of linguistics.

Further Reading

Artandi, Susan. "Machine Indexing: Linguistic and Semiotic Implications." *Journal of the American Society for Information Science* 27:235–239 (1976).

Cornog, Martha. "A History of Indexing Technology." *The Indexer* 13:152–157 (1983).

Grishman, Ralph. "Natural Language Processing." *Journal of the American Society for Information Science* 35:291–296 (1984).

Janas, Jurgens M. "Automatic Recognition of the Part-of-Speech for English Text." *Information Processing and Management* 13:205–213 (1977).

Slobin, Dan Isaac. *Psycholinguistics.* Berkeley: University of California, 1979.

Wellisch, Hans H. "'Index': The Word, Its History, Meanings and Usages." *The Indexer* 13:146–151 (1983).

The Arrangement and Retrieval of Information

CHAPTER

4

Information Storage and Retrieval

Susan Bonzi

Computer technology has introduced many possibilities in the storage and re-trieval of information. Many of the concepts which underlie the traditional meth-ods used in libraries are also the basis for computerized storage and retrieval techniques. But in addition, the speed and storage capacities of modern comput-ers allow for much more flexibility in searching for information than was ever feasible with manual systems.

An information storage and retrieval system consists of several components, including (1) a storage device; (2) the organization of the information; (3) the representation or form which the information takes; and (4) a searching mecha-nism to permit retrieval. In traditional libraries, the storage device is usually the book or journal, located on shelves within the physical structure of the library building. The information is organized according to some classification scheme, e.g., Dewey Decimal or Library of Congress. Most of the information is in printed form, and is usually complete in itself—that is, the entire document (e.g., book or journal article) is present. Finally, common searching mechanisms in-clude the card catalog and indexes to journal literature.

In computerized information storage and retrieval systems, the storage device is the computer itself. Both documents and their locations are stored within the computer. The machine presents only a copy of the document to the user, so the user's ability to physically locate a given item need not be a consideration in the organization of the collection. Therefore, since computerized information is not constrained by physical location, much greater flexibility in organization of the information is feasible. The representation of information in a computerized system is likely to be a reference to a full document rather than the complete text itself, although there are many databases which do contain complete information within them. Searching a computerized system may be as straightforward as searching for a subject or author in a card catalog or index. However, computer-ized searching allows for much more complex searches to be performed.

In this chapter, three of the four components of an information storage and retrieval system outlined above will be discussed in light of modern technology. The first component, the storage device, will not be discussed because an adequate

39

discussion of computers would be quite lengthy. There are many introductory texts on the subject. References to a few of them are given at the end of this chapter.

Organization of Information

There are many ways of storing information, but one of the prerequisites is that the information must be organized in a way that it can be easily located. The ease of finding a particular item is dependent on a variety of factors, particularly on the size of the collection of items to be searched and the way a person approaches the collection. Three common methods of organizing material are presented here.

Unordered Files

If a collection of items is very small, there is rarely any need to organize the items for purposes of retrieving a specific one. For example, in a record collection consisting of twenty albums, finding one of the twenty is not difficult at all. Even examining every record would not be very time consuming. On the average, a person would have to look through just about half of the records in order to find the one wanted. The first record might be the one desired, but it is just as likely that the desired record will be the last. In searching through an unordered file, the average number of items to be searched is equal to (n minus 1)/2, where n equals the total number of items. If the collection consists of twenty items, the average number of records needed to be searched is (20 minus 1)/2, or 9.5 records. However, if the collection consists of 200 items, some order may become necessary. In a collection of 200 items, the average number of items to be scanned is just about 100, a number large enough to make the search very time consuming, at least for a human. Computers, because of the speed with which they work, could search 100 or even 1,000 items very quickly. But very large files, consisting of hundreds of thousands of items, would be slow work, and there are much more efficient ways of searching.

Sequential Files

One of the simplest methods of ordering larger files is the sequential method. In a sequential file, each item is in order, usually alphabetically or numerically. The white pages of a telephone directory is an obvious example of sequential order. Sequential order works quite well as long as the items are ordered according to the way people will search. For example, the telephone directory works extremely well as long as the person searching knows the name of the person he or she wishes to call. If only the address is known, however, a standard telephone directory is virtually useless.

Searching a sequential file can be much less time consuming than searching an unordered file. Humans searching a sequential file (e.g., a telephone book, a dictionary, or a card catalog) usually have a good notion of the approximate location of the item desired, and start from there. By jumping backwards and forwards from the initial point, they soon find what they are looking for, providing it is there. In a large file, this method is obviously far more efficient than

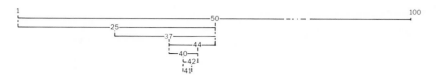

Figure 4.1. Binary search for the number 41

looking at each item in order. A computer can be programmed to search a sequential file in much the same manner as a human would, thus making the search much more efficient than searching the file record by record.

The most efficient method of searching a sequential file by computer is the binary search. A binary search is somewhat like a typical human search of a sequential file, but because the computer cannot think, it cannot make an educated estimate of where to start looking. Its best guess is to start at the middle. In a binary search, the file is divided in half, and the item sought is compared with the midpoint. If the midpoint is not the item sought, then a comparison is made to see if the item is in the first half or in the second half. For example, if the last name Franklin is sought in an alphabetical list of names and the last name Moore is at the midpoint, Franklin would be in the first half because it occurs earlier in the alphabet. The half in which the name would not appear is ignored. The half in which the item would appear is then divided in half and another comparison is made to determine whether it is in the first half or the second half of the initial half being considered. The new portion of the file in which the item would appear is again split in half, and the process continues until the exact point where the item either is or should be is found. Although this strategy seems tedious, any item in a sequential file of 1,000 items can be found in only 10 tries. In a file of 1,000,000 items, the desired item can be found in a maximum of 20 tries. Figure 4.1 illustrates a binary search for the number 41 in a sequentially ordered file of 100 numbers.

Although sequential files are preferable to unordered files, there are two major disadvantages in their use. The first, as noted above, is that they are easily searched from only one access point, such as name. The second disadvantage is that if a record is added to the file, insertion of the record in the proper order entails rewriting of the file. The third method of ordering files, the inverted file method, has neither of these disadvantages.

Inverted Files

An inverted file structure consists of two parts. The first part is a file of records which may or may not be ordered. The second part is the inversion of the main file. It consists of a group of indexes which includes potential aspects of the records to be searched, e.g., author or title. Each entry in the index includes keys which tell where records containing the desired information may be located. The keys may be likened to the page numbers given for subjects in a book index, citations to articles in a journal index, or call numbers on catalog cards. The keys in inverted files give the locations of each item in the computerized file. In computerized bibliographic retrieval systems, there are indexes for author, journal, date of publication, descriptors (the controlled subject vocabulary), and free text terms, which include all significant words in the title and in the abstract, if there is one. The entries in each index are alphabetically arranged, and each entry in an index has the location or locations of each item in the file which pertains to the entry in the index.

As an example, let us assume that a person wants all articles written by Frederick Humphreys. Let us also assume that Document 6742 is a reference to an article by Humphreys titled "Recent Research in the Use of Emergency Rooms by Indigents." In the author index, which is in alphabetical order, there will be an entry for "Humphreys, Frederick." With that entry will be the location in the computer of Document 6742, which gives the complete citation of the article. A search for articles by Humphreys will take place in the author index. Since the author index is in alphabetical order, the computer will do a binary search of the index until it finds Humphreys' name. It will then read the location of each article by Humphreys (in this case, only one), go to that location, and retrieve a copy of the reference for the searcher to see. If the searcher wants all articles with the word "indigents" in the title, the computer will do a binary search on the title index, which is an alphabetical list of every significant word in every title, until it finds the word "indigent." It will then read the locations of all references in which the word appears (one of which will be Humphreys' article), make a copy of each, and present them to the user.

When a document is added to an inverted file, it can be simply added to the end of the file. The indexes are then updated, adding the location of the document to appropriate existing terms in the index and adding new terms when needed. The indexes may need to be reordered and rewritten, but the main file of documents do not. This is much more efficient since the indexes are relatively small compared with the main file.

Representation of Information

In modern information storage and retrieval systems, information is represented in one of two forms, either in full text, that is, the complete text of the documents, or as a document surrogate. The document surrogate is a reference to the complete text. The majority of commercially available databases contain only document surrogates, and of these, most are representations of bibliographic works, e.g., journal articles, dissertations, books, and technical reports. A document surrogate usually contains a bibliographic citation to the work, an abstract of the work, and a number of descriptors from a controlled vocabulary which are used to describe the work.

Controlled Vocabulary

The controlled vocabulary is a set of terms which has been chosen to represent the subject matter of the discipline. The purpose of a controlled vocabulary is to bring the language of the authors of documents in an information storage and retrieval system and the language of the users of the system together. For example, the user of the system may want information on teachers. The author of a highly relevant document in the system, however, may use the word "instructors" instead of the word "teachers." The controlled vocabulary may include the term "educators" in its list of acceptable terms, with cross references from both "teachers" and "instructors." The indexer of the document, then, seeing that it concerns the concept of instructors, would assign the term "educators" as a descriptor because the controlled vocabulary directs him from "instructors" to "educators." The user of the system, seeing that "teachers" is not an accepted controlled vocabulary term but that "educators" is, would then use the accepted term in searching for suitable documents.

The main reason for a controlled vocabulary is to control synonyms, but there are other advantages to using a controlled vocabulary as well. Homonyms, those words that are spelled alike but differ in meaning, are also controlled by the inclusion of a note explaining the scope of the term, by other terms associated with it, or merely by inclusion in a vocabulary developed for one subject (the term "ring" in a chemical vocabulary would obviously have the chemical meaning). In addition, the problem of false coordination is avoided. For example, if a searcher entered the terms "library" and "school" in order to find items about library schools, the chances are very good that many items on school libraries would also be retrieved. But use of the controlled term "library school" would retrieve only items on library schools. Controlled vocabularies may also give the scope of certain terms which are unclear in meaning, thus clearing up possible ambiguities.

Controlled vocabularies can range in structure from a simple list of terms used for description of documents to the highly structured thesaurus, which organizes the terms in a hierarchical fashion. In a thesaurus, each term in the vocabulary is shown in relation to other terms like it. The term may be more specific in nature than another term, e.g., the term "secondary schools" is more specific than the term "schools." In this case, the entry in the thesaurus for "secondary schools" will show the broader term (usually abbreviated to BT) "schools." Likewise, the term "junior high schools" is more specific than the term "secondary schools." This narrower term (NT) would also be included in the entry for "secondary schools." There would also be entries for "schools" with "secondary schools" listed as NT, and for "junior high schools" with "secondary schools" listed as BT.

Those terms in a thesaurus which belong to more than one hierarchy will have more than one broader term shown in the entry. More common, though, are terms which belong to only one hierarchy. There may, however, be many narrower terms for any one broader term. An obvious example is the term "languages," which may have several individual languages listed as narrower terms.

In addition to broader and narrower terms, a particular thesaurus entry may also show a variety of terms which do not specifically fit into the hierarchy but

Secondary Schools

BT: Schools

NT: Junior High School
High School
Middle School

RT: Funding-Secondary Schools
Enrollment-Secondary Schools
Instruction-Secondary Schools

SYN: Secondary Education

Figure 4.2. Secondary schools as a sample thesaurus entry of a controlled vocabulary

are in some way related. These related terms (RT) may show any of a variety of relationships between two terms, e.g., cause and effect or process and product.

Entries in a thesaurus also include any terms which could have been used in place of the entry term. The terms are usually synonymous with the entry term and are included only to direct the user to the accepted term. An example of an entry in a controlled vocabulary thesaurus is given in Figure 4.2.

Thesauruses are difficult and time consuming to construct, but they have several advantages over simple lists of indexing terms. Because they show the hierarchical relationships among terms, the degree of specificity allowed in the vocabulary is easily ascertained. The display of broader and narrower terms gives clues as to how to proceed if an initial search strategy is too narrow or too broad in scope. The display of related terms, as well as broader and narrower terms, provides other terms which the searcher may not have considered in the initial preparation of a search strategy.

Natural Language

In addition to controlled vocabulary terms assigned to a document, the intellectual content of a document is also represented by the title, abstract, or in fulltext databases, by the text itself. These are the natural language elements of the document, not controlled by a specific vocabulary of terms. In most databases, the natural language of the document can be searched, and there are both disadvantages and advantages in doing so. One disadvantage in natural language searching is the increase in the possibility of false coordination (e.g., the difference between items dealing with "library school" as opposed to "school library"). Another disadvantage is that the searcher may not think of all of the relevant terms which might have been used by authors to describe a concept. Thus, many relevant documents may be missed. If the person needing information is very familiar with the concepts of interest, however, he or she will probably know all, or at least the most commonly used, terms which are likely to occur in the documents sought. Homonyms may also present a problem, but usually the context of the search statement will weed out any documents using an ambiguous term in an entirely different manner from what is intended.

One advantage in using natural language in searching is that it allows the search to be as specific as the author of the document has been. For example, if a person needs information on the feeding habits of robins and the controlled vocabulary is no more specific than "birds," the use of the controlled vocabulary term may retrieve irrelevant documents. However, if the natural language of the author is searched, the chances of retrieving only documents on robins are much better. The use of natural language in searching is particularly important when a relatively new concept is of interest, one which has not found its way into the controlled vocabulary.

Although the use of controlled vocabularies can be very valuable as well as preferable in many situations, tests comparing natural language searching with controlled vocabulary searching have shown that natural language is at least as good as and generally superior to searching with a controlled vocabulary.

Retrieval of Information

When information on a simple topic is needed, it should be relatively easy to find, providing, of course, that the information storage and retrieval system has documents relating to the topic. For example, if a person needs information on libraries, there should be little problem, as long as the term "libraries" or something very like it is a searchable term. Likewise, a person needing information on schools should find that information listed under the heading "schools" or a synonym. But a problem arises when a person wants information on a more specific or more complex topic, e.g., library schools. He or she may have to look under every entry for "schools" in order to find those few which deal with library schools, and may also need to look under the term "libraries" in order to find any others.

Precoordinate Indexing

This problem has traditionally been solved by foreseeing likely combinations of ideas and adding them to the indexing vocabulary. The method of putting ideas together at the indexing stage is called precoordinated indexing because the ideas are coordinated together before the system is used. The problem with precoordinated indexing is that many ideas which involve more than one concept cannot be foreseen. For those which have not been precoordinated, the user may go through a great deal of effort before retrieving the desired information.

Postcoordinate Indexing

A solution to the problem of searching complex topics is postcoordinate indexing. With this type of indexing, individual terms are assigned to documents, but instead of being coordinated at the time of indexing, they are coordinated at the time of searching. Thus, the name postcoordinate indexing.

Several postcoordinate indexing schemes have been developed. The Uniterm

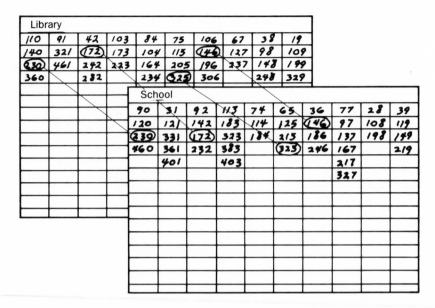

Figure 4.3. Uniterm type cards

system, developed by Taube in 1951, is described here because it is conceptually very similar to the inverted file structures used in modern information retrieval systems.

In Taube's system, each term used to represent a concept is written on a separate card. The card also contains the identification numbers of all documents which deal with the concept. If two concepts are to be coordinated together, the searcher chooses the appropriate cards and compares the document numbers on the first card with those on the second. Those numbers which appear on both cards should deal with the topic of interest. Figure 4.3 illustrates the coordination of "library" and "school."

Modern information storage and retrieval systems which use inverted files are very much like Taube's Uniterm system. The terms are located in machine-readable indexes rather than on cards, and the computer, rather than the searcher, checks for matches. But the idea of assigning document identification numbers to terms and then checking the terms for appropriate documents is essentially the same.

Postcoordination of terms allows much greater flexibility in searching than does precoordination. One problem is that of false coordination. In many operational information retrieval systems, this problem can be overcome by specifying word order. For example, if the searcher specifies that the term "library" must precede the term "school," then "school library" will not meet the search specifications. Requiring the use of additional command language, however, places an added burden on the searcher.

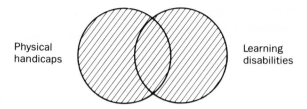

Figure 4.4. Illustration of Boolean OR logic: physical handicaps OR learning disabilities

Boolean Logic

Today, the most common method of searching computerized stores of information is with symbolic logic, which was invented in the nineteenth century by the mathematician George Boole. Symbolic logic, more commonly known as Boolean logic, basically consists of three operations: the logical sum, the logical product, and the logical difference.

In Boolean logic, the logical sum is the total of one set of items plus the total of another set of items. For example, a person might request "documents containing information on physical handicaps and documents containing information on learning disabilities." Interestingly, the request would not be stated as "physical handicaps AND learning disabilities," but rather as "physical handicaps OR learning disabilities." This is because the requester does not necessarily want documents containing information on both physical handicaps and learning disabilities. What he or she wants are documents containing information on either physical handicaps or learning disabilities. Some documents may contain information on physical handicaps alone, some may contain information on learning disabilities alone, and, of course, some may contain information on both subjects. The requester should be satisfied with any of the documents. Figure 4.4 illustrates the logical sum, represented by the Boolean OR operator. This figure, along with Figures 4.5, 4.6, and 4.7, graphically represents the relation between the terms with Venn diagrams, developed by Jon Venn to illustrate Boolean logic.

The logical product is the intersection of one set of items with another set of items. Only those which meet both requirements are satisfactory. If the request

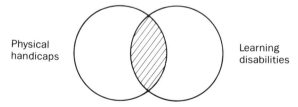

Figure 4.5. Illustration of Boolean AND logic: physical handicaps AND learning disabilities

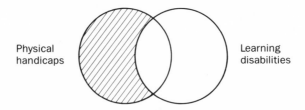

Physical
handicaps

Learning
disabilities

Figure 4.6. Illustration of Boolean NOT logic: physical handicaps NOT learning
disabilities

had been "documents containing information on both physical handicaps and learning disabilities," then the logical product, represented by AND, would be used, since both concepts must be present in order to satisfy the request. The request would be stated as "physical handicaps AND, learning disabilities," and is illustrated in Figure 4.5.

The logical difference is the set of items containing one characteristic but not those items containing another characteristic. For example, if the request is "information on physical handicaps but no documents dealing with learning disabilities," the search statement would be "physical handicaps NOT learning disabilities." The retrieved set of documents satisfying this request would not contain any documents dealing with learning disabilities, even though they may also deal with physical handicaps. Because it may delete relevant information, the NOT operator is potentially dangerous. It is used much less often than either AND or OR. Figure 4.6 illustrates the Boolean NOT.

More complex strategies may be developed by using combinations of Boolean operators. For example, if the request is "information on educational programs for either physical handicaps or learning disabilities," the request might be stated as "educational programs AND (physical handicaps OR learning disabilities)." The parentheses are included in this statement because without them, it is unclear

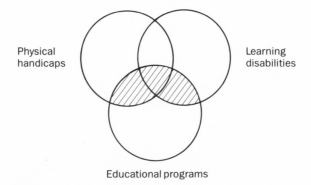

Physical
handicaps

Learning
disabilities

Educational programs

Figure 4.7. Illustration of combined logic: educational programs AND (physical handicaps OR learning disabilities)

whether the request is for information on either (educational programs and physical handicaps) or learning disabilities, or it is for information on educational programs and either (physical handicaps or learning disabilities). Figure 4.7 illustrates the search combining "educational programs" with the other two concepts.

There is an order of precedence in operational information storage and retrieval systems which determines which operations (AND, OR, NOT) are executed before the others. The order of precedence used within the system can be overridden by the use of parentheses.

Term Weighting

Retrieving information by using Boolean logic involves both terms representing concepts of interest and the relationships among those terms. There are other methods of retrieving information which ignore any logical relationships among the concepts of interest. Probably the most common method is term weighting.

The idea of term weighting relies on the supposition that the frequency of occurrence of a term within a document is correlated with the degree to which that document is about the concept represented by the term. For example, if the term "helicopter" occurs three times in a document, it is probably about helicopters to a greater extent than is a document in which the term "helicopter" occurs only once. The simplest way to implement the concept is by measuring within document frequency (WDF). This measurement is calculated for each significant term within the document. (Those words which occur very frequently in text, e.g., "the," "and," "if," etc., are called stop words and are usually ignored by the system.) In the search process, terms from the user's query are then matched to each document, and those documents with a large number of occurrences of query terms found in the document are retrieved.

Term weighting also allows the ranking of documents which are retrieved. Those documents with the highest score (the highest frequency of all terms in the query) are presented first. Documents with lower scores are placed further down on the list. In Boolean retrieval, there can be no ranking of documents because the decision to retrieve is based solely on the presence or absence of terms, regardless of their frequency. However, with WDF and other weighting schemes, some documents may be more "about" a topic of interest (measured by the frequency of occurrence of the terms) than others, and can be presented in order of "aboutness."

A more complex term weighting scheme involves the use of inverse document frequency (IDF). This method also calculates the number of occurrences of each term in each document, but in addition, it considers the frequency of occurrence of each term across all documents in the collection. If a term occurs 5 times within a document and only 100 times in all documents within the collection, the frequency of occurrence in the document probably indicates that the document deals with the concept represented by the term to a large extent, at least as compared to other documents in the collection. However, if the term occurs 5 times in a document and 10,000 times within the collection (as could easily be the case for the term "education" in an educational database), the significance of that frequency within the document is much less. One method of calculating inverse document frequency is by dividing the frequency of a term within the document by its frequency within the entire collection.

As an illustration, consider a query containing the terms "soil" and "erosion." In one document, "soil" occurs 5 times, and "erosion" occurs 2 times. In another document, "soil" occurs 2 times, and "erosion" occurs 7 times. With a system that uses only WDF, the second document would be considered as more "about" the query than the first, since the query terms appeared a total of 9 times in the second and 7 times in the first. However, if "soil" occurs 100 times in the collection, and "erosion" occurs 1,000 times in the collection, the first document would be ranked above the second when IDF is calculated. In the first document, "soil" would get an inverse document frequency score of .05 (5/100), and "erosion" would get a score of .002 (2/1000), for a total score of .052. In the second document, the score for "soil" would be .02 (2/100), and the score for "erosion" would be .007 (7/1000), for a total score of .027. Thus, taking the frequency of occurrence of terms across the entire collection can change the ranking of documents in response to a particular query.

Relevance Feedback

Relevance feedback is a method which attempts to improve on the set of documents initially retrieved by an information storage and retrieval system. In a system utilizing relevance feedback, the user is presented with a set of documents in response to a request. The user reviews the documents retrieved and decides which of them are relevant. The system then analyzes the relevant documents, usually by frequency of occurrence of terms, although other methods of analysis may also be employed. The system then uses the results of the analysis to search for more potentially relevant documents in the database. The new set of documents is presented to the user, who may be satisfied with the new set or may direct the system to continue the process until he or she is satisfied.

Summary

Modern information storage and retrieval systems use computers to store information. The information within the computer may be organized in any of a number of ways, but since most files are quite large and need to be accessed in a variety of ways, inverted structures are most commonly used. The information may be represented either by controlled vocabularies, e.g., thesauruses, and by the natural language of the author or abstracter. Most retrieval systems provide the capacity to use Boolean logic in searching, but a few allow other methods, e.g., term weighting, and may even provide such enhancements as relevance feedback.

Further Reading

Computer Technology

Bohl, Marilyn. *Information Processing*. 4th ed. Chicago: Science Research Associates, 1984.

Hopper, Grace Murray and Steven L. Mandell. *Understanding Computers*. St. Paul, Minn.: West Publishing, 1984.

Shelly, Gary B. and Thomas J. Cashman. *Computer Fundamentals for an Information Age*. Brea, Calif.: Anaheim Publishing, 1984.

Stern, Robert A. and Nancy Stern. *An Introduction to Computers and Information Processing*. 2nd ed. New York: John Wiley & Sons, 1985.

Information Storage and Retrieval

Lancaster, F. Wilfrid. *Information Retrieval Systems: Characteristics, Testing, and Evaluation*. 2nd ed. New York: John Wiley & Sons, 1979.

Salton, Gerard and Michael J. McGill. *Introduction to Modern Information Retrieval*. New York: McGraw-Hill, 1983.

Van Rijsbergen, C. J. *Information Retrieval*. 2nd ed. London: Butterworths, 1979.

5

Database Design and Management

Carol Tenopir

Librarians have used online bibliographic database searching for well over a decade. Good searchers are familiar with the content and characteristics of individual databases (such as ERIC or Chemical Abstracts) and with the online system (e.g., DIALOG or BRS) and the commands that are needed to search each database. Searchers must also have an understanding of how databases are created and structured, how they are processed by the online system's computer to enable searching, and what actually happens when a database is searched. This chapter focuses on these issues. Chapter 6 discusses specific databases and systems.

Databases

There are many definitions of "database"; in a broad sense, online databases, such as those used by libraries, are merely collections of related information made searchable on computer. These collections are most often related by subject (e.g., information about education or about chemistry); by type of information (e.g., books, dissertations, journal articles); or by issuing agency (e.g., materials created by the U.S. Government Printing Office).

A majority of the databases used in libraries today are bibliographic (also called indexing/abstracting) databases. Bibliographic databases provide citations to literature just as printed indexing tools do. Sometimes abstracts are also available. Bibliographic databases serve as pointers to books, articles, proceedings, research reports, or audiovisual materials; the user must then locate the full document referred to in the bibliographic citations, just as he or she must locate the books in the library after searching the library catalog. Online citations are often called "document surrogates" or "document representations" because they substitute for or describe the actual document.

A typical bibliographic database is composed of from 5,000 to over 1 million individual records, which are surrogates to the corresponding documents. Figure 5.1 is an example of records from two databases that are available on the DIALOG search service. Each record is made up of a series of fields, representing one piece of information describing some particular aspect of a document. The first

BIBLIOGRAPHIC   Each record in a bibliographic database is a reference or citation (many also include a summary or abstract) to a publication, magazine or journal article, news story, patent, conference paper, etc.

```
File  47:MAGAZINE INDEX  (Copr. IAC)

Alexandria archeology. (Alexandria, Virginia)
Early American Life  v18  p39(3)  April  1987
CODEN: EALIDQ
illustration; photograph; chart
GEOGRAPHIC CODE: NNUSUVA
GEOGRAPHIC LOCATION: Virginia
CAPTIONS: (Plan of Alexandria, Virginia drawn by George Washington.)
DESCRIPTORS: Alexandria, Virginia--antiquities; Archaeology--Virginia
```

```
File  16:PROMT  (Copr. Predicasts Inc. 1987)

    Can US processors sell to Japanese buyers?.
Plastics World   March 1987   p. 33-36

    US plastics processors may be able to tap a potential market of over 2
million passenger cars/yr made by foreign-based firms, according to Philip
Townsend Assoc. By 1990, 5 more Japanese and 1 S Korean firm will assemble
cars in the US and Canada due to a nearly 40% rise in the value of the yen
vs the dollar, eliminating much of the traditional price advantage enjoyed
by Japanese imports, and the possibility of import quotas on assembled
vehicles or local content laws that would reduce exports of parts for
assembly in the US. Japanese investment is also induced by over $20 billion
worth of economic incentives offered by states and municipalities. In
addition, 30 Japanese producers of nonautomotive products will start up
plants in the US by 1988, according to G Farris of Borg-Warner Chemicals.
The Townsend study found 50 Japanese producers of plastic or elastomic
parts now operating in the US or planning to do so, and expects the number
of plastics-related plants to rise to 100-150 by 1990.
    The Japanese customer-supplier relationship is characterized by loyalty;
once a firm becomes a supplier, it can expect a long-term relationship.
Japanese technical and administrative teams (often at a high executive
level) repeatedly visit the potential supplier to thoroughly examine the
plant and evaluate management, asking about the firm's balance sheet, cost
structure and other financial matters that many US businessmen consider
proprietary. Since Japanese assembly plants operate with a 1-shift
inventory on many items and change colors or models several times/shift, a
supplier's delivery reliability and production flexibility are scrutinized.
Article discusses Honda's vendor-screening procedures. Nissan's
requirements of parts suppliers and joint ventures.

*1USA *United States *3075210 *Plastic Automotive Parts *24 *marketing
1USA United States 3711100 Automobiles 46 use of materials
```

Source: DIALOG System Seminar (Palo Alto, Calif.: DIALOG Information Services, 1985). Reprinted by permission.

Figure 5.1. Bibliographic records

record in Figure 5.1 has ten fields—title, journal name, collation, year of publication, CODEN, special features (e.g., illustration), geographic code, geographic location, captions, and descriptors. Together these fields provide a surrogate of the original document.

Fields are often divided into subfields, discrete items of information within any given field. In the collation field, for example, there are subfields for volume number, issue number, pagination, and month of publication. The descriptor field in this example has two individual descriptors, each of which can be considered a subfield of the major descriptor field. Subfields may or may not be searchable online depending on the decision made by the database producer and online vendor.

Subfields may be broken down into data elements, the smallest searchable unit within a database record. Each word in the title, abstract, descriptor, or identifier fields may be a separate data element or keyword when each can be searched individually.

Other types of databases are used less frequently in libraries, but their availability and use are increasing each year. Fulltext databases provide complete articles or books online instead of merely a surrogate. In most online systems, the complete document (except graphics) can be searched and retrieved online. Full texts of most U.S. legal statutes, many popular magazines, several encyclopedias, and assorted journals and textbooks are now available online. Figure 5.2 is an example of two shortened records from two fulltext databases.

Numeric or statistical databases provide different types of numeric data including census data, financial information, economic/labor data, physical or chemical properties, and the like. Some online systems allow this data to be manipulated to create such things as forecasting reports. The nature of the data in numeric databases varies widely, but Figure 5.3 illustrates one typical type available on the DIALOG system.

Referral (or directory) databases lead the user to a person, company, or product. Telephone "yellow pages" directories, biographical sources, and other referral sources such as software directories, periodical directories, and database directories are now widely available online. Figure 5.4 contains a referral database illustration.

Most of the databases available in the 1980s computerized versions of printed works. Beginning in the late 1960s, many publishers of printed indexing and abstracting tools began using computer typesetting to create their print products. Computer typesetting enhanced and expedited the printing process; it also resulted in a computer-readable magnetic tape version of the work. This version, when loaded onto a computer with appropriate searching software, provided a potential source of extra income to the database producer by allowing enhanced search and retrieval and wider distribution of the product.

Many types of publishers now make their products available as online databases. Government agencies, professional societies, large for-profit publishing firms, small entrepreneurial publishers, and academic institutions all create databases.

Typically, databases are leased from publishers by online vendors, such as DIALOG or BRS (also called online systems or hosts), who make the databases available for searching. The vendor has a computer or computers, massive amounts of disk storage, and software for making databases available for searching. The vendors also take responsibility for marketing the services, billing clients, and making arrangements with telecommunications networks that are used by searchers to access online systems over the telephone lines. Database producers are responsible for the content of their databases, while most online

FULL-TEXT Records in a full-text database include the complete text of magazine articles, newswire stories, encyclopedias, etc.

```
File 648:TRADE AND INDUSTRY ASAP  (Copr. IAC 1988)

Tokyo's stock market: stronger than you think. (includes related article on
  what to buy in Tokyo market)
Curran, John J.
Fortune  v117 p76(5) April 11, 1988
CODEN: FORTA
illustration; photograph; graph
AVAILABILITY: FULL TEXT Online  LINE COUNT: 00271
SIC CODE: 6231
CAPTIONS: Japan, US, UK stock prices Sept. 1987-March 1988.
COMPANY NAME(S): Tokyo Stock Exchange--evaluation
DESCRIPTORS: Stock-exchange--Analysis; Securities--prices

     WESTERN INVESTORS have been worrying about the Tokyo stock market,
which many consider, to adapt a phrase, a riddle wrapped in an enigma, with
a dash of inscrutability thrown in. Share prices that seemed high before
Black Monday have now practically climbed back to where they were before
the crash. Will Tokyo lead the way down next time, dragging the whole world
with it? Not likely. The Japanese market is not as overvalued as you may
think.

     What's the evidence, you ask? Japan's economy is booming, yet
inflation remains at what Americans would consider a satisfying creep.
After a two-year lull, corporate profits are surging. Domestic spending has
increased sharply, making up partly for the drop in exports induced by the
rising yen. Tokyo's high-priced Ginza shopping district, once a mecca for
tourists, now bustles with Japan's own legion of consumers. The country's
GNP charged ahead at a 7% rate in the fourth quarter of 1987, a big
surprise to Western forecasters who thought the strong yen would strangle
growth.

     Does all that mean you should buy in? Perhaps -- but with caution, not
gusto. No bull market lasts forever, and Tokyo's has been chugging along
       .            .          .              .
       .            .          .              .
       .            .          .              .
```

```
File 600:McGraw-Hill News (Copr. 1988 McGraw-Hill, Inc.)

OPEC OIL OUTPUT ROSE TO 18.2 MLN BBLS/DAY IN APRIL, IEA REPORTS
Gulf states boost production despite rise in gulf hostilities

DATE:  May 6, 1988      17:19 E.T.     WORD COUNT:  235

     McGRAW-HILL NEWS (Paris)  --The   Organization   of   Petroleum  Exporti
Countries's  crude oil production shot up to some 18.2 million barrels a day
April  from  17.7  million  bbls/day  in March, the International Energy Agen
said.

     The  IEA  Monthly  Oil  Market  report  said  Persian  Gulf  states rais
production despite the recent increase in hostilities in the gulf.

     Iraq,  Iran,  Saudi Arabia, and United Arab Emirates are projected to ha
raised production by 100,000 bbls/day each, the report said.

     OPEC  production  averaged  17.5  million bbls/day in the first quarter
       .            .          .              .
       .            .          .              .
       .            .          .              .
```

Source: DIALOG System Seminar (Palo Alto, Calif.: DIALOG Information Services, 1985). Reprinted by permission.

Figure 5.2. Fulltext records

vendors merely take the information as submitted and process it so it can be searched. (In some cases the database "producer" and online "vendor" are the same company. H. W. Wilson Company, for example, both produces and vends its own databases.)

NUMERIC Each record in a numeric database is a table of statistical data, often with text added.

```
File 565:ECONBASE   (Copr. 1988 The WEFA Group)

AUTO RETAIL SALES, NEW IMPORTED CARS, UNITED STATES

    Series Code:   USCARIMP
    Corp Source:   BEA ;  UNPUBLISHED DATA
    Start Date:    JANUARY, 1967 (6701)
    Frequency:     MONTHLY
    Units:         MILLIONS, SEASONALLY ADJUSTED ANNUAL RATE

    1988   JAN   3.104    FEB   3.082    MAR   3.005
           APR   3.24
    1987   JAN   2.501    FEB   2.99     MAR   2.906
           APR   3.046    MAY   2.959    JUN   3.084
           JUL   3.311    AUG   3.721    SEP   3.757
           OCT   3.343    NOV   3.257    DEC   3.436
    1986   JAN   2.948    FEB   2.924    MAR   2.881
           APR   3.167    MAY   3.053    JUN   2.968
           JUL   3.272    AUG   3.334    SEP   3.763
           OCT   3.26     NOV   3.407    DEC   3.841
    1985   JAN   2.558    FEB   2.566    MAR   2.347
           APR   2.501    MAY   2.854    JUN   2.801
           JUL   2.917    AUG   2.909    SEP   3.077
      .            .            .            .          .
      .            .            .            .          .
      .            .            .            .          .
    1968   JAN   .956     FEB   .995     MAR   1.004
           APR   .966     MAY   .976     JUN   1.002
           JUL   1.024    AUG   1.015    SEP   1.21
           OCT   1.081    NOV   1.058    DEC   1.07
    1967   JAN   .629     FEB   .69      MAR   .742
           APR   .748     MAY   .784     JUN   .787
           JUL   .814     AUG   .817     SEP   .803
           OCT   .806     NOV   .852     DEC   .892
```

Source: DIALOG System Seminar (Palo Alto, Calif.: DIALOG Information Services, 1985). Reprinted by permission.

Figure 5.3. Numeric records

Since the middle to late 1970s, when database searching became widespread, more and more databases have been created expressly for the online market rather than as byproducts of a print technology. Creating a database can be a time-consuming task, even when it is derived from an existing product. The fact that online search tactics differ from manual techniques must be considered when creating an online product. Database producers thus must make a series of decisions as they convert their data to a format acceptable to the online system and as they attempt to make their database the best possible online searching tool.

New database producers (electronic publishers) are faced with the creation of the intellectual work as well as with formatting issues. Database design decisions can be divided into these two major areas: (1) creation (intellectual) decisions, and (2) implementation (software-related or structural) decisions.

DIRECTORY Each record in a directory database gives factual information about companies, organizations, products, etc.

```
File 516:D & B - Duns Market Identifiers  (Copr. 1988 D&B)

UNIVERSITY PATENTS INC                  Full financials available
1465 POST ROAD EAST
PO BOX 901
WESTPORT, CT   06881

TELEPHONE: 203-255-6044
FAIRFIELD COUNTY        SMSA: 418  (NORWALK,CONN)

BUSINESS: PATENT BUYING, LICENSING & LEASING, MFR CONTACT LENSES

PRIMARY SIC:    6794       PATENT OWNERS/LESSORS
SECONDARY SIC:  3851       OPHTHALMIC GOODS
SECONDARY SIC:  7391       RESEARCH & DVPT LABS
SECONDARY SIC:  7392       MGMT & PUB. RELATIONS
SECONDARY SIC:  0751       LIVESTOCK SVCS X SPEC
SECONDARY SIC:  5199       NONDURABLE GOODS

YEAR STARTED:            1964

                    CURRENT          TREND          BASE
                    YEAR             YEAR           YEAR
                                     (1985)         (1982)

SALES ($):          1,620,000        1,620,000      2,520,000
EMPLOYEES TOTAL:          110               99             25
EMPLOYEES HERE:            20

    SALES GROWTH (%):      - 36
    EMPLOYMENT GROWTH (%): 296

SQUARE FOOTAGE: 12,000  RENTED
NUMBER OF ACCOUNTS: 1,000
BANK: PUTNAM TRUST OF GREENWICH INC
ACCOUNTING FIRM: COOPERS & LYBRAND

THIS IS:

    A HEADQUARTERS LOCATION
    A CORPORATION
    A PUBLIC COMPANY
    A MILLION DOLLAR DIRECTORY COMPANY

DUNS NUMBER:            04-929-4093
HEADQUARTER DUNS:      04-929-4093
CORPORATE FAMILY DUNS: 04-929-4093

CHAIRMAN:              MILES, L. W.   / CHAIRMAN OF THE BOARD
PRESIDENT:            ALPERT, A. S.  / PRESIDENT
VICE PRESIDENT:      KOFFSKY, DAVID  / VICE PRESIDENT
VICE PRESIDENT:      MC PIKE, FRANK R.  / VICE PRESIDENT
SECRETARY:           ROBERT, I. S.  / SECRETARY
MARKETING:           SIEGEL, ROBERT I.  / V P - MARKETING
OPERATIONS:          FRIANT, RAY J. JR. / V P - OPERATIONS
FINANCE:             MCPIKE, FRANK R. JR. / V P - FINANCE
```

Source: DIALOG System Seminar (Palo Alto, Calif.: DIALOG Information Services, 1985). Reprinted by permission.

Figure 5.4. Referral records

Creation Decisions

A librarian searching a database is probably more cognizant of the creation decisions than the implementation decisions. Creation decisions directly affect the quality of the material distributed by the intermediary to clients. Like printed reference sources, databases must be evaluated for content and quality—two things that the database producer has control over.

Creation decisions can be broken down into content decisions, standardization decisions, decisions about value-added fields, and quality control decisions. Together, these decisions will determine how useful and how reliable a database is.

Content of a bibliographic database or a printed index involves decisions on what materials are indexed and to what extent. A publisher of an indexing tool must decide whether to index just journals or just books, or to include materials such as research reports, dissertations, audiovisuals, proceedings, government documents, etc. Sometimes these decisions define the nature of the work (e.g., Conference Proceedings Index or Dissertation Abstracts), but often they become an editorial policy. The type of materials retrieved in a search is, of course, an important consideration for the intermediary who perhaps must supply the original documents to the end user. The publisher of a printed index decides whether all of the types of materials included in the print version will also be available online. Because of the high cost of printing, some online databases include more records online than in the printed counterparts. It is helpful for the searcher to know upon what criteria this selection is based.

Knowing what materials are included in a database does not tell the entire story of content. Index and database producers make a decision about how comprehensively they cover their materials. Very few indexing/abstracting tools include real "cover-to-cover" indexing of journals, for example. Most exclude advertisements, letters to the editor, and other ephemeral materials. Some producers selectively choose articles from a number of journals, while others include all articles from a list of journals. Selection can be based on subject matter, length of the articles, or quality. Many databases concentrate on English language materials only. Figure 5.5 is an example of some content decisions of one database producer.

Standardization is an issue that may not be noticed in a printed tool but becomes much more crucial in an online product because online searching is a literal process. That is, computers cannot think or make educated assumptions. The online system's software matches a string of characters that the searcher inputs as a search term. Most software on the major online systems is not sophisticated enough to catch spelling variations (e.g., to recognize the difference between "Labour" and "Labor") or variations in format. In these cases it is to the searcher's advantage to have the contents of the database as standardized as possible. Nonsubject fields that a publisher can control at the creation stage include dates (January 1977 vs. 1/77), places (Chicago, IL vs. Chicago), names (Jones, John B. vs. Jones JB), abbreviations (assoc. vs. association), and spelling. (Some software features aid the searcher dealing with nonstandardized database content. These are discussed below.)

A related content decision is that of value-added fields. Value-added fields include anything added to the basic bibliographic record to aid retrieval or enhance the material retrieved. Typical value-added fields in a bibliographic database include descriptor terms, abstracts, and codes. Codes might represent

---

Editorial Policy

The editorial policy of **sa** is based on three criteria: *inclusiveness* — to abstract the entire range of sociological journals and those in related disciplines irrespective of language of publication; *systematicity* — to abstract fully every core sociological journal and select from related journals those articles directly pertinent to sociology and those written by sociologists; and *continuity* — to abstract journals in chronological sequence of their publication whenever possible.

On the basis of the above criteria, three *types* of journals have been distinguished in the following order of priority:

Type 1 — journals published by sociological associations, groups, faculties and institutes, and periodicals containing the term sociology in their titles;

Type 2 — journals from such related areas as anthropology, economics, education, medicine, community development, philosophy, statistics, political science, etc.; and

Type 3 — journals from the humanities and journals of general circulation wherein scholars and laymen publish discussions or criticisms of sociology and sociological topics.

Records in **Sociological Abstracts** consist of:

	85%	journal articles (with abstracts online since 1973);
less than	10%	conference papers (1969–1972, citations and index entries only online; print product contains citations, index entries, and abstracts) (1973–1976, print issues only; 1977 forward, citations and abstracts, print and online.)
less than	5%	books (to 1963, citations and index entries)

Source: Sociological Abstracts (San Diego, Calif.).

Figure 5.5. Editorial policy of a database producer

taxonomic families, subject classification numbers, Standard Industrial Classification codes, etc.

The number and quality of the value-added fields in a particular database often set it apart from other databases in the same subject. These fields provide additional access points to increase the number of documents retrieved. Standardization or control of these fields helps improve precision and recall by imposing a consistent vocabulary on all records in the database. The value and role of controlled vocabulary are discussed in Chapter 4.

Quality control impacts the way searchers input search terms and affects the number of citations retrieved. The simplest level of quality control is checking for and correcting typographical errors. If a word in a record is misspelled it will not be retrieved in the normal search process. Some database producers verify the information at input, while others will correct errors reported to them. Since many databases are updated only monthly, there may be quite a lag between when an error is discovered and when it is corrected. Correcting errors can be expensive also.

Other types of quality control are more complex. Eliminating outdated information and verifying the accuracy or quality of the articles indexed are factors that greatly impact the services that are provided. It is more expensive for a database producer to exercise this level of quality control, a fact that may be reflected in the price of the quality database. If information from an online search is inaccurate, is the intermediary (such as a company that produces an initial index), the database producer, or the online vendor responsible? This issue of liability is expected to arise increasingly as there is more reliance on online sources and as intermediaries charge for online searches.

Implementation Decisions

File Structures

When the magnetic tape of a database is received by the online vendor from the database producer, the database must be processed (or "loaded") onto the vendor's computer. Each record is stored in accession number order in what is called the linear, sequential, or unit record file. Figure 5.6 could be two records in the linear file of one database.

If the linear file was the only way records were stored in an online system, searching would be done sequentially by having the computer look at each record in turn (like looking for a particular song on a cassette tape). In a sequential database search, the system would look for a given string of characters, character-by-character through each record in a database. Such sequential scanning is possible (and some software for creating small in-house databases works this way), but it would be very time consuming in a large database. (Imagine searching for the term "library" in the printed ERIC indexes *Resources in Education* and *Current Index to Journals in Education* by starting at the first character in the first record and continuing to scan each of the 500 to 1,000 characters per record in all of the close to a million entries.)

Instead of relying on sequential scanning of the linear file, it is more efficient with today's still-limited computer technology to have the computer create a separate file that stores just the searchable data elements from each record with pointers back to the appropriate unit record in the linear file.[1]

In most online systems today, such inverted files (or indexes) are derived from the linear file when the database is loaded by the online vendor. Some systems maintain more than one inverted file—separating the subject-related fields into a default "basic index." Two types of inverted files from the DIALOG system are illustrated in Figure 5.6. An inverted file can be thought of as an index to the searchable words or phrases in each record in a database. Each term is extracted automatically from each record and placed in an alphabetically ordered list. Each term in this list contains a numerical pointer to another file that contains information about each term. This information typically includes the accession number of each record that contains the term, the fields where the term is found in each

---

1. Specially designed computer hardware is being developed for rapid scanning of computer files, thus making possible search and retrieval of large databases without the need of inverted indexes. Although early versions of these "database machines" are now available, they are not yet widely used.

---

1. DIALOG assigns consecutive ACCESSION NUMBERS to all records received in machine-readable form, creating a LINEAR FILE, where the complete records are stored.

30249   (accession number)

Postpurchase   consumer   evaluations,   complaint   actions   and   repurchase
 TI1   TI2   TI3   TI4   TI5   TI7
behavior.
 TI8

Francken, Dick A.
 AU

Journal of Economic Psychology,   1984 Nov Vol 4(3) 273-290
 JN   PY

Language: ENGLISH   Document Type: JOURNAL ARTICLE
     LA   DT

Presents a model of postpurchase evaluation processes, which is used as a
 AB1 AB2 AB3   AB5   AB6   AB7   AB8 AB9 AB10 AB11 AB12
theoretical   framework for explaining different kinds of consumer complaint
 AB13   AB14   AB16   AB17   AB18   AB20   AB21
actions.
 AB22

Descriptors: CONSUMER   ATTITUDES   (11470);   CONSUMER BEHAVIOR (11480)
      DE1   DE2   DC   DE3   DE4 DC

30156   (accession number)

Labor   force   participation   of metropolitan,   nonmetropolitan, and farm
 TI1   TI2   TI3   TI5   TI6   TI8
women: A comparative study.
 TI9 TI10 TI11   TI12

Bokemeier, Janet L.; Sachs, Carolyn; Keith, Verna
 AU   AU   AU

Rural Sociology,   1984 Win Vol 48(4) 515-539
 JN   PY

Language: ENGLISH   Document Type: JOURNAL ARTICLE
     LA   DT

Examined   data   from 937 metropolitan, 3631   nonfarm-nonmetropolitan, and
 AB1   AB2   AB4   AB5   AB6   AB7   AB8
1231   farm   women   (18-65   yrs   of age) from Kentucky to compare personal,
 AB10 AB11 AB12 AB13 AB14 AB15   AB17   AB19   AB21 AB22
socioeconomic,   and   family   characteristics and the occupations and
 AB23   AB25   AB26   AB29
industries of women in the labor force.
 AB31   AB33 AB34 AB36 AB37

Descriptors: EMPLOYMENT   STATUS   (17196);   HUMAN FEMALES (23450);   URBAN
      DE1   DE2   DC   DE3   DE4 DC   DE5
ENVIRONMENTS   (54940);   RURAL   ENVIRONMENTS (45040)
 DE6   DC   DE7   DE8   DC

LINEAR FILE (vertical label, left margin)

Source: DIALOG System Seminar (Palo Alto, Calif.: DIALOG Information Services, 1985). Reprinted by permission.

Figure 5.6. Database construction

record, and the placement of each term in each field (e.g., the 5th word in the title field in the 500th record).

Inverted file structures greatly speed up searching, because when a user searches for a term, the system goes to the alphabetically arranged inverted file rather than scanning the complete linear file. (This process is somewhat analogous to checking the cover of a record album to decide which band has the

> 2. DIALOG creates the database's BASIC INDEX, the alphabetical list of subject words (excluding STOP WORDS). Each record is divided into FIELDS (parts), each field is labelled, and the position of each word within a field is noted.

a	30249 ·AB2	in	30156 AB34
	30249 AB12	industries	30156 AB31
	30156 TI10	is	30249 AB9
actions	30249 AB22	kentucky	30156 AB19
	30249 TI5	kinds	30249 AB18
age	30156 AB17	labor	30156 AB36
as	30249 AB11		30156 TI1
attitudes	30249 DE2	metropolitan	30156 AB5
behavior	30249 DE4		30156 TI5
	30249 TI8	model	30249 AB3
characteristics	30156 AB26	nonfarm	30156 AB7
comparative	30156 TI11	nonmetropolitan	30156 AB8
compare	30156 AB21		30156 TI6
complaint	30249 AB21	occupations	30156 AB29
	30249 TI4	participation	30156 TI3

STOP WORDS		
an	for	the
and	from	to
by	of	with

> 3. DIALOG creates the database's ADDITIONAL INDEXES of remaining searchable fields. These indexes are searched with PREFIXES.

AU=Bokemeier, Janet L.	30156
AU=Francken, Dick A.	30249
AU=Keith, Verna	30156
AU=Sachs, Carolyn	30156
DC=11470	30249
DC=11480	30249
DC=17196	30156
DC=23450	30156
DC=45040	30156
DC=54940	30156
DT=Journal Article	30249
	30156
JN=Journal of Economic Psychology	30249
JN=Rural Sociology	30156
LA=English	30249
	30156
PY=1984	30249
	30156

Figure 5.6. cont.

desired song, then going directly to that band.) Using the index, the retrieval system first reports the number of records that contain a search term (called "hits" or "postings"). The accession numbers for the records that satisfy a given search request are put into a separate numbered group called "a set." Sets are created for each search term or for each search statement entered. Not until the searcher enters a display command does the system use the accession numbers

```
?b 75
     22mar85 12:35:50 User003842
$0.13    0.005 Hrs File1
$0.03  Dialnet
$0.16  Estimated cost this file
```

```
File  75:Management Contents - 74-85/Feb
(Copr. 1985 Information Access Co.)
```

```
     Set    Items   Description
     ---    -----   -----------
?ss turnover or job?(w)satisfaction or employee?(w)morale?
     S1      1077   TURNOVER
     S2     12532   JOB?
     S3      3219   SATISFACTION
     S4      1779   JOB? (W)SATISFACTION
     S5     16063   EMPLOYEE?
     S6       796   MORALE?
     S7       147   EMPLOYEE?(W)MORALE?
     S8      2820   TURNOVER OR JOB?(W)SATISFACTION OR EMPLOYEE?(W)MORALE?
```

```
?ss flextime or flexitime or flexible (w)work?(w)schedule?
     S9        75   FLEXTIME
     S10       40   FLEXITIME
     S11     1715   FLEXIBLE
     S12    22659   WORK?
     S13     1863   SCHEDULE?
     S14       19   FLEXIBLE(W)WORK?(W)SCHEDULE?
     S15      114   FLEXTIME OR FLEXITIME OR FLEXIBLE(W)WORK?(W)SCHEDULE?
```

```
?ss s8 and s15
            2820   S8
             114   S15
     S16      30   S8 AND S15
```

Where:

```
     S =  Set
     Items =  Hits or Postings
     (w)    =  with, proximity search
     ss     =  Select Set
     ?      =  Suffix Search
```

Source: DIALOG System Seminar (Palo Alto, Calif.: DIALOG Information Services, 1985). Reprinted by permission.

Figure 5.7. Typical search on the DIALOG System

stored in the set to access the linear file records. See Figure 5.7 for a typical search, and Figure 5.8 for an example of a print display of a search.

When a database is first made available on an online system, the database producer and online vendor together make certain decisions about the database structure. Individual fields in the records are defined. The fields that are to be searchable are so designated for inclusion in the inverted files. Field tags and subfield delimiters are added to the records. The field tags differentiate between fields for the inverted file creation program and tell where one field ends and the next begins. Subfield delimiters tell the programs where one subfield ends and the next begins.

One of the most important decisions at this stage is how each field or subfield

```
?t 16/5/1-2

16/5/1
289478      SPM84D0010
  Effectively Managing Alternative Work Options.
  Olsten, W.
  Supervisory Management, Vol.24, No.4, April 1984, P. 10-15., Journal.
  Alternative work schedules are popular with employees. For alternative
work options to function effectively, the manager must develop specific
strategies. (Flexible work schedules) can result in higher productivity and
positive (employee morale.) The new work styles can be beneficial to the
company only when the manager is prepared to handle potential problems. The
manager must develop a strategy that includes hiring practices, work plan,
performance   goals,   training   program,   managerial   support,   and   open
communications.  There are different systems of alternative work schedules,
and a manager must evaluate the appropriate system for his firm.

  DESCRIPTORS:  Management; Flexible Schedule; (Flextime; Work Hours; Strategy;
Productivity; Morale; 0605; 0173; 0173; 2427; 0251; 0662; 0240

16/5/2
287779      SPM84B0037
  Taking a Look at (Flexitime).
  Morgan, P.I.; Baker, H.K.
  Supervisory Management, Vol.29, No.2, Feb. 1984, P. 37-43., Journal.
  Many  companies  are  allowing  employees  to  establish  alternative  work
scheduling.  The concept of flexitime is encouraged to reduce absenteeism and
job (turnover), and encourage (job satisfaction) and productivity.  Flexitime
originated in Munich, Germany in 1967. An experiment related to flex-time is
the compressed forty-hour work week. The organization receives the benefits
of employee satisfaction and effectiveness from flexitime.  Employees derive
personal benefits from flexitime.  Flexitime should only be adapted when a
correct implementation procedure is followed, and when it is determined that
the concept is advantageous to the organization.

  DESCRIPTORS: (Flextime; Work Hours; Work Week; Absenteeism; (Turnover); Job
Satisfaction; Employee;  Productivity; Organization; Implementation; Benefits;
0173; 2427; 2431; 0058; 0429; 0221; 0958; 0662; 0576; 1641; 1057
```

NOTE: The search did not retrieve the terms "flexible schedule" or
        "flex-time" (underlined). It did not retrieve the term "flexible
        schedule" because we only asked for instances of "flexible work
        schedule"; it did not retrieve the term "flex-time" because the system
        views this as a different word than "flextime".

Source: DIALOG System Seminar (Palo Alto, Calif.: DIALOG Information Services, 1985). Reprinted by permission.

Figure 5.8. Print display on the DIALOG System

will be processed for the inverted indexes. Each field will be machine "indexed" ("parsed") by some specified criteria. Parsing is the process of identifying how each record, field, subfield, and data element will be separated and making entries in the inverted index for each separate part. How a field is parsed is important because it greatly affects how the words or terms in a record can be searched.

There are three parsing options available for a database. A different option can be chosen for each field in a database if desired.

"Word parsing" (word indexing) is the approach used for many subject-related fields in many databases. A word is usually defined as any string of letters or numbers that is bounded by blank spaces or punctuation marks. To parse a word-indexed field, the system creates a separate entry in the inverted index each time a word is encountered. Thus, the title *Developing Computer-Based Library*

Systems would have five separate alphabetically arranged entries in the inverted index: BASED, COMPUTER, DEVELOPING, LIBRARY, and SYSTEMS.

Most online systems have a list of trivial words ("stop words") that are not included in the inverted indexes. Stop words typically include prepositions such as "of" and "with," articles such as "an" and "the," and conjunctions such as "and," "or," and "but" (although the number of words designated as stop words varies among the online systems).

When the computer creates the inverted index, it checks the stop word list and does not make an entry for any word on the list. Thus, the title *In Search of Excellence* would have only two entries in the inverted index of most systems: EXCELLENCE and SEARCH.

Many systems retain word placement information about the stop words, however, so the system would note that "excellence" was the fourth word in the title of this record and "search" was the second word. The significance of this placement information will be discussed later.

Word parsing is the approach typically chosen for noncontrolled fields such as title, abstract, and fulltext. It means that the word-parsed field can be searched by every nontrivial word that it contains.

"Phrase parsing" (phrase indexing) is usually used for controlled fields where a human indexer has indicated that the words in a phrase go together as a "bound" phrase. Phrase-parsed entries in the inverted indexes include all spaces and punctuation. The computer software can detect where one phrase ends and another begins because the index terms have been marked with a special delimiter.

The author field is often phrase parsed. In the first record in Figure 5.2, the author, "Curran, John J.," would generate only one entry in the inverted index. That entry would be exactly as the phrase was entered in the database: CURRAN, JOHN J., including all spaces and punctuation.

Phrase parsing keeps bound terms together, but it greatly impacts searching. The entire phrase must be searched in order to retrieve the record. Thus, in a search for this author the user must know to input "Curran, John J." exactly as shown (Curran comma space John space J period). Neither "Curran" nor "John" alone would retrieve this record. Most systems have search features that aid searching phrase-parsed fields. These are discussed below.

"Combination-parsed" fields ("double posted") are both word and phrase parsed. Bound phrases are kept together, but they are also separated at spaces and punctuation. This approach is typically used in the descriptor or identifier fields where there are bound ("precoordinated") phrases but where individual words are also meaningful.

Double posting is nice for the user because it retains the intellectual decision involved in creating a bound descriptor, yet it allows individual words to be searched when a user may not know the correct form of a bound term.

The second record in Figure 5.6 has the major descriptors: EMPLOYMENT STATUS; HUMAN FEMALES; URBAN ENVIRONMENTS; and RURAL ENVIRONMENTS. Here the semicolon (;) indicates to the system where one bound descriptor subfield ends. For these four descriptors the system might make twelve separate entries in the inverted index if the field were both phrase and word parsed. The entries would be:

EMPLOYMENT
EMPLOYMENT STATUS
ENVIRONMENTS (2)
FEMALES
HUMAN
HUMAN FEMALES
RURAL
RURAL ENVIRONMENTS
STATUS
URBAN
URBAN ENVIRONMENTS

Combination parsing, as you can see, allows the most flexibility for the searcher but also creates the longest inverted index that uses the most space in the computer.

Implications for Searching

As mentioned earlier, implementation decisions have a direct impact on how a database can be searched. Word-indexed fields can be searched on individual words, phrase-indexed fields on complete phrases only, and a field that is indexed by a combination can be searched by either words or complete phrases.

Online systems usually have several searching features that provide more flexibility in searching fields regardless of how they are parsed. These features include: truncation, the ability to view the inverted index online, proximity searching, Boolean logic, and the ability to specify a particular field.

Most online systems allow the searcher to use word stem "truncation" search for all terms or phrases that begin with the same character stem. The stem is usually indicated to the system by a special truncation symbol. Thus, putting a truncation symbol after the stem "librar" will find entries in the inverted index under LIBRARY, LIBRARIES, LIBRARIANSHIP, LIBRARY AUTOMA-TION, etc. The truncation symbol varies with the system. It is variously designated as a #, ?, :, $, etc.

Truncation is especially valuable for phrase-indexed fields because it will allow a searcher to retrieve records without knowing the complete phrase. Searching for the author LANCASTER$ will retrieve all records that include any author with the last name Lancaster. The searcher does not have to enter the spacing, punctuation, or initials exactly right because they all come after the truncation symbol. This search might, however, result in some "false drops" (irrelevant records) because it will retrieve all authors with the last name Lancaster.

Most major online systems allow the user to view parts of the alphabetic inverted index online. By looking at the inverted index, the searcher can see what words or phrases are available for searching, see the many term variations that occur especially in uncontrolled fields, and find the exact phrase and format that must be entered to search a phrase-indexed field. This can help eliminate false drops caused by truncation.

An especially powerful feature for searching word-indexed fields is "proximity searching," available on many online systems. Proximity searching allows a searcher to "postcoordinate" phrases from word-indexed fields such as titles or abstracts. This is possible because of the positional information that is recorded by the online system at the time the inverted index is created. The positional information indicates the field and where in the field each term occurs. A user can ask, for example, for the word "library" right next to the word "automation" in any word-indexed or double-posted field. The system will use the positional information to reconstruct the phrase even though each word is entered separately in the inverted index.

Proximity features vary among systems. Some typical capabilities include the ability to specify: words adjacent to each other (as illustrated above), words with a specified number of intervening words, words in the same sentence, words in the same paragraph or field.

Boolean logic searching is another form of postcoordination, but it works at the document level rather than at the field level. The main Boolean operators AND, OR, and NOT are described in Chapter 4. They allow words or phrases from any fields in a document to be linked together by the searcher. AND designates that both terms must be present in the same record, OR designates that either term may be present, and NOT excludes records that have a specified term. Boolean logic searching is facilitated by the existence of the inverted index. All logical operations are performed using the information in the inverted index.

Some online systems provide some help with inconsistent word forms by providing look-up tables for common equivalencies. Although not widely available, this includes equivalency tables for British and American spelling variations, Chinese Romanization schemes, corporate source acronyms and complete forms, and common abbreviations (e.g., Nov. for November). Currently, all of these are available only on Mead Data Central's systems such as LEXIS and NEXIS. When a user enters one form or another of the look-up table terms the system will automatically check all documents for either form of the term. On Mead Data Central's systems it is done without informing the user ("transparently" to the user).

Other online systems (notably H. W. Wilson's WILSONLINE) provide automatic look-ups and searching for controlled vocabulary descriptors. If an incorrect form of a descriptor is entered the system will automatically search for the correct descriptor instead. In the case of WILSONLINE, the system informs the user of the extended search.

Such automatic look-up (termed "mapping") takes part of the burden of search strategy from the searcher. It aids the database producer as well, by substituting for the costly practice of standardization at input.

A final common system search feature that is made possible by the database design and construction conventions discussed in this chapter is the ability to specify particular fields for searching. Most online systems allow the searcher to limit a search to a particular field or fields. This ability speeds searching time and reduces the number of false drops. A search of WHITE$ on only the author field, for example, will eliminate entries with subject words such as "white-wash," "whitewalls," etc. Searching AUTOMATION only as a descriptor or title word will avoid retrieving records where the term was used just in passing in an abstract or full text. Field specification thus allows more precision in searching. It can also be used in some systems in the printing of search results. A searcher can choose which fields in the database records to print, making the final printout a more customized product.

Summary

Database design involves two levels of decision making: creation (intellectual) decisions and implementation (structural) decisions. Creation decisions are made by the database producer and include content, standardization, value-added fields, and quality control decisions. They vary widely among database producers. Implementation decisions are in part dependent on the software of the online system that makes the database available for searching. Implementation decisions include identifying the fields in each record and deciding how each field will be parsed (entered into the system's inverted indexes).

Both creation and implementation decisions impact searching. The quality and amount of information retrieved are in part dependent on creation issues. Search conventions in online system software (e.g., truncation, viewing the inverted index, word proximity, Boolean logic, term mapping, and field specification) together with the implementation decisions have a direct effect on the success of an online search.

Further Reading

Chen, Ching-Chih and Peter Hernon, eds. *Numeric Databases.* Norwood, N.J.: Ablex, 1984.

Fenichel, Carol H. "Process of Searching Online Bibliographic Databases: A Review of Research." *Library Research* 2:107–127 (Summer 1980).

Mintz, Anne. "Online Databases and Liability." *Library Journal* 110:38–43 (September 15, 1985).

"Numeric Databases." *Drexel Library Quarterly* 18 (Summer-Fall 1982). Has 12 papers on the topic.

Palmer, Roger C. *Online Reference and Information Retrieval.* Littleton, Colo.: Libraries Unlimited, Inc., 1983. 2nd ed., 1986.

Tenopir, Carol. "Databases: Catching Up and Keeping Up." *Library Journal* 109:180–182 (February 1983). Lists recommended textbooks and articles written in 1982 and before.

————. "Full-Text Databases." In Martha E. Williams, ed. *Annual Review of Information Science and Technology.* 19th ed., 215–246. Washington, D.C.: American Society for Information Science, 1984.

Williams, Martha E. "Electronic Databases." *Science* 228:445–456 (April 26, 1985).

CHAPTER

6

Online Database Searching

Christyn Billinsky

Online database searching was first available for library use in the early 1970s. Though it is a relatively recent development in the library and information world, online searching has already had a tremendous impact on the ways in which people seek and use information. In 1972 there were about 40 databases available online; by 1987 that number had increased to over 2,800. This tremendous increase marks the beginning of a major trend to use computers for the storing and retrieval of information.

Databases, Vendors, and Retrieval Software

In order for online searching to be a cost-effective reality, several key ingredients were required: interactive computers with reasonably priced processing and direct access disk storage capabilities, databases, retrieval software, and telecommunications networks. By the early 1970s all of these key ingredients were developed and in place.

The beginnings of database development are rooted in improvements introduced to the typesetting of index and abstract publications during the 1960s. Traditionally a typesetter worked directly with a typesetting machine to produce photo-ready pages for publication. The early 1960s brought the introduction of computer typesetting where the material was typed (or keyboarded) into a computer. The computer would then process (sort and format) the data and send it to computer-driven typesetting equipment, which then produced the typeset pages ready for publication. Beyond improving the production cycle for printed abstracts and indexes, computer-assisted typesetting created computer databases. The information contained in the printed abstracts and indexes was now stored in machine (computer) readable form and directly available to the tremendous processing powers of the computer.

Early databases were generally the machine-readable equivalent of the printed index and abstract publications. Today many databases offer enhanced information when compared to their print counterparts, and some databases have no print counterparts at all and are available only online. While early databases were primarily bibliographic databases, containing only citations and possibly abstracts, some databases today are fulltext databases that contain the entire text of the materials in the file. These databases can be a tremendous help in searching for extremely specific information. Other forms of databases are sometimes called fact or numeric databases because they contain the actual information sought rather than a reference to a source that might contain the needed information. Examples are census, statistical, economic, and stock market databases. Some traditional reference tools such as directories, handbooks, and encyclopedias are also now available as online databases.

At the same time that databases were being created, various groups of researchers were working on developing retrieval software to enable effective searching of the computer databases. Two of the first developers were Lockheed and SDC. Both worked under government contract, Lockheed to develop a retrieval system for NASA and SDC to develop a retrieval for the National Library of Medicine. In 1972 both SDC and Lockheed (now DIALOG Information Services) began direct commercial service of their own, making several databases publicly available for online searching. In 1976 BRS joined the group of online vendors offering lower-cost services that were targeted at the academic library market. The BRS retrieval system was based on a package called STAIRS that had been developed by IBM. BRS added significant enhancements to make searching both simpler and more flexible.

H. W. Wilson joined the ranks of online vendors in 1985 with the introduction of its own online retrieval system, WILSONLINE. Wilson decided not to provide its databases to the established vendors, but rather to develop a system of its own. The various Wilson indexes are available online only through Wilsonline.

Most initial databases were in the area of science and technology (ERIC was the major exception), and most users were special libraries serving government or corporate scientific research and development. As costs decreased and the subject range of databases expanded to include business, social science, and humanities information, the user community also expanded to include business, academic, public, and, finally, school libraries.

In 1979, as personal computers started to appear in homes and offices, two new online vendors appeared in the marketplace, The Source and Compuserve. The Source was aimed primarily at individual users while Compuserve was aimed at both small business and individual users. This development was a significant change from the services of DIALOG, SDC, and BRS that were primarily designed for use by trained searchers in a library or other information setting. Both Compuserve and The Source offered low-cost evening rates to help promote use by individuals.

Traditional online vendors that had been used extensively by libraries saw an opportunity to expand their market to include end users with personal computers in their homes or offices. Both DIALOG and BRS designed and marketed alternative retrieval systems aimed specifically at personal computer users in the individual home or office. DIALOG developed Knowledge Index, and BRS developed BRS After Dark and then BRS Breakthru.

Generally, the alternative services offered reduced rates for evening searching and either a simplified search language or a menu-driven search protocol to make searching easier for the end user searcher. H. W. Wilson chose a slightly different approach to attract end user searchers and designed a special software package to use with a personal computer when searching WILSONLINE. The package, called WILSEARCH, lets the user search WILSONLINE as a menu-driven system. An experienced searcher usually finds that the alternative retrieval systems lack some of the speed, flexibility, and power of the standard retrieval systems. The alternative systems do however simplify the search process for end user searchers doing such things as compiling term paper bibliographies, locating a specific fact, or finding reading materials to use as background for a presentation. Software that enables simplified searching is still in its first generation, but as each new package or service is used and evaluated, progress toward simpler yet more powerful systems is made.

Equipment and Software for Online Searching

The vendors of online databases have large computers on which they make databases available for searching by users throughout the world. Though there are variations on the specifics of how the searches take place, a typical method is as follows.

Database producers enter information directly into their own computers. From this information they will create whatever printed products they market and also a tape that they send to the online database vendor. Upon receiving the tape the online database vendor mounts it on a computer tape drive and runs it against formatting and indexing programs to create the database and indexes that will be accessed by the online searchers. When processing is finished, the database and indexes are then stored on computer disk drives to enable fast retrieval.

Online searchers can now access the vendor's computer, generally through a telecommunications network. The telecommunications networks lease telephone lines throughout the nation, which they then make available to computer users at rates that are lower than direct long-distance dialing. A searcher usually dials a local number to get access into the network, and then tells the network which online vendor he or she wants to access. At that point the network establishes a link between the searcher and the vendor for the duration of the search.

Until the early 1980s the most common equipment used for online searching was a computer terminal equipped with a modem. A computer terminal is a device that lets an individual communicate with a computer. A modem alters the signals sent from the terminal so that they can be efficiently carried long distances over telecommunications lines. Since a printed copy of search output is almost always necessary, either a printing terminal or a CRT terminal with an attached printer was most typically used. While simple to use and reasonably inexpensive, the computer terminal does not provide much in the way of flexibility. It simply prints out the searcher's search statements and the computer's search output line by line as the search session progresses. If any reformatting of search output is desired, either a cut and paste operation or a complete retyping of search output is necessary.

The early 1980s brought the introduction of the microcomputer as a sophisticated online searching machine. The microcomputer provides new power and capabilities for online searching procedures. With appropriate software the searcher can perform a variety of operations that saves both time and money, and makes possible the offering of enhanced information services. Among the possibilities are:

1. Automation of the various log-on procedures.
2. Typing in search strategies offline to send to the host system at a later time (uploading).
3. Capturing and saving the search results on disk (downloading).
4. Reformatting the downloaded search results for custom bibliography production.
5. Creating in-house databases from the downloaded search.

In order to use a microcomputer for online searching there are several hardware and software requirements that must be met. The microcomputer needs to have:

1. An RS232C serial port—some microcomputers come with built-in serial ports; however, for most microcomputers a separate communications card with serial port must be purchased.
2. One and preferably two floppy disk drives—floppy disks are used to upload and download, and then later to reformat saved search output.
3. A modem—there are three possibilities: (a) built-in modems come with some microcomputers, especially the portables; (b) internal modems are built onto circuit board cards that are placed inside the microcomputer. Generally the internal modem card contains both the modem and the RS232C serial port; and (c) external modems sit outside the computer and require an RS232C cable to connect with the RS232C serial port.
4. A printer—although theoretically optional, a printer is almost essential.
5. Communications software—the communications software program is that which enables the microcomputer to function as a terminal. Different programs offer different features. As a minimum a searcher would generally want communications software that will: (a) automate the log-on procedure; (b) upload; (c) download; (d) control the printer; (e) break or interrupt output; and (f) interface with a wordprocessing software package for reformatting downloaded saved output.

It is essential that the various online searching components be designed for compatibility. The modem and printer must be compatible with the computer, and searching will go much more smoothly if the communications software explicitly supports both the modem and printer. Before the components are purchased, if at all possible, it is advisable to witness their operation in configuration. A minimum precaution would be to check with current users to determine what type of equipment and software they use and what kinds of experiences they have had. Also, making contact with one of the many online users groups can be one of the most useful things that librarians new to online searching can do.

One of the major reasons for using the microcomputer for online searching is that the search results can be saved to disk for later editing into a polished bibliography, or for inclusion in an in-house database. In order to do these things, additional software is required. While wordprocessing software can enable one to manipulate and format the saved search output into a clean bibliography, most general purpose wordprocessing software is not designed to fully facilitate the process. For instance most wordprocessing software does not have a sorting capability. If sorting cannot be done on the host system before the search output is downloaded there will need to be a number of rather tedious movings of citations in order to produce a sorted bibliography. Also, wordprocessing software does not automatically produce specially formatted citations. If the citations of the bibliography need to be in a format other than that provided by the host, there is no magic key to push that will change the citations from their current format into the desired format. With general purpose wordprocessing packages a lot of very tedious effort is required to reformat the bibliography from its raw downloaded form to the final polished format.

Software products that facilitate the reformatting of downloaded search output for bibliography production and in-house databases began to appear in the mid-1980s. Generally the process of downloading and reformatting is divided into three steps, which will usually involve the use of three software packages or three modules of one integrated package. First, a communications software package is used to perform the search, download, and save the raw search output. Another software package (or module) will then be used to convert the raw search output into the format required by the database package (the third piece of software). Once the newly formatted material has been loaded into a file by the database package, the user can easily manipulate the material for bibliography production, special report preparation, or further searching.

One example of specialized downloading and reformatting software is a series of packages marketed by Personal Bibliographic Software, Inc. (PBS). The total package involves three separate pieces of software: Prosearch, Bibliolink, and Pro-Cite. Prosearch is a communications package that performs downloading, and also includes many features that can help to simplify the search process. Bibliolink converts the downloaded output into the format required by Pro-Cite, the database package. There are several Bibliolink packages; each one converts and reformats material from a specific online vendor (i.e., there are separate Bibliolink packages for working with DIALOG, BRS, OCLC, and RLIN). An institution that searched both DIALOG and BRS would therefore require two Bibliolink packages, one for use with DIALOG and one for use with BRS. Once material is loaded into Pro-Cite, the user can easily create custom formatted bibliographies and reports, or perform further searching of the newly created in-house database.

When considering the purchase of downloading and reformatting software, plan to see it in operation before buying. Determine what kind of effort and how many steps are required in order to convert the raw search output into the in-house database or specially formatted bibliography. Selecting the software to use in conjunction with online searching is as important a task as selecting the microcomputer and modem, because it is through the software that one works with downloaded search output. It is the software that determines how much subsequent effort will be required to convert the downloaded search output into the in-house database or custom bibliography.

The Search Process and Sample Search

The major vendors of online databases all base their retrieval systems on the AND, OR, and NOT of Boolean logic. Though each vendor employs a different command language, the underlying logic for strategy construction is the same from vendor to vendor. The sample search that is provided in this section uses the DIALOG search system.

Online searching has all the variety and diversity that is typical of traditional reference work. The major difference is that the user consults computer databases to locate information rather than the traditional printed sources. Just as the traditional reference librarian needs to know the organization and content of the individual printed reference works, the online reference librarian needs to know the organization and content of the individual databases.

As in any reference work, online work has both simple and complex information requests. The sample search in this section demonstrates a simple search performed in a bibliographic database (i.e., a database that contains bibliographic citations). For this sample search the user wants to find citations to general interest articles concerning nutrition for the elderly.

The first step is to determine what databases to search. Since the user wants articles of general interest, the search will be run in Magazine Index, a file that indexes popular general-interest journals.

The second step is to look at the topic and break it into its logical concept areas. This topic has two concept areas: nutrition and elderly. The chances are reasonably good that if the citation to the article contains both the words "nutrition" and "elderly" the article itself will deal with the topic of nutrition for the elderly.

The third step is to think of alternative ways that the topic might be expressed. For instance, the term "diet" could be included in the nutrition concept area, and the term "aged" included in the elderly concept area. If variant word endings are acceptable for some of the terms, one should also designate the significant word stem to be searched. Several databases have a thesaurus of vocabulary terms that should be consulted when deciding what terms to include in a search strategy.

Some people find Venn diagrams a help in visualizing search strategies at this point. Figure 6.1 shows the Venn diagrams for this sample search.

OR Connector

Used to group
synonymous terms
when <u>at least one</u>
must be present.

Nutrition or Diet

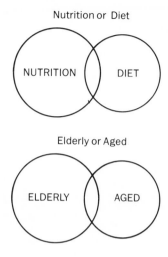

Elderly or Aged

AND Connector

Used to connect
concepts or terms when
<u>both</u> or <u>all</u> must be
present.

(Nutrition or Diet) AND (Elderly or Aged)

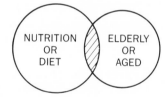

Source: Based on *DIALOG System Seminar* (Palo Alto, Calif.: DIALOG Information Services, 1987). Reprinted by permission.

Figure 6.1. Venn diagrams showing logic for sample search: nutrition for the elderly

Search worksheets are generally used as a tool to help structure search strategy development. The sample worksheet included here as Figure 6.2 notes the topic, databases to be searched, concept areas of the search, and the words or word stems to be included in the concept areas.

The fourth step is to formulate the strategy into the language of the search system. Once this step is completed it is time to go online and perform the search. A copy of the online session as executed on the DIALOG system is included as Figure 6.3. The underlined material is what the searcher keyed in; all of the other material is computer response.

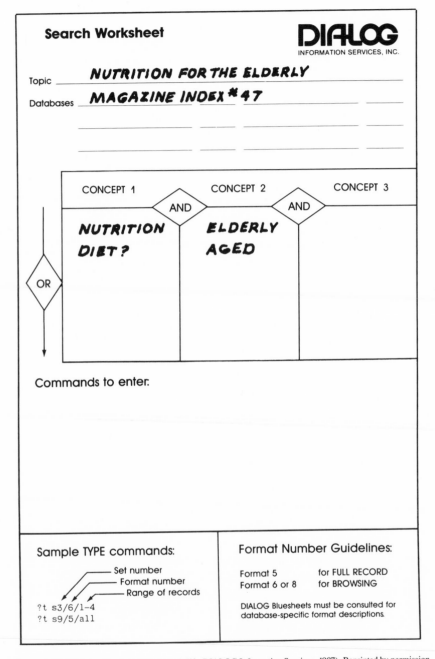

Figure 6.2. Sample search request form

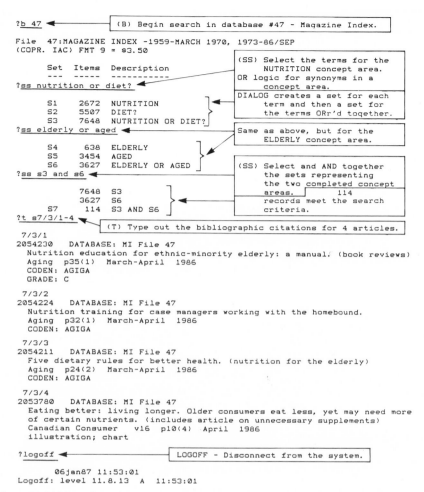

Source: DIALOG System Seminar (Palo Alto, Calif.: DIALOG Information Services, 1987). Reprinted by permission.

Figure 6.3. Sample search on the DIALOG system: nutrition for the elderly

All online searching is not this straightforward. The simple sample search is intended to show a basic approach that is often used in searching bibliographic databases. As with traditional reference work, some requests are simple and others are complex. To do a good job of online searching the searcher must have a thorough knowledge of the databases—just as the traditional reference librarian has known the printed materials on the shelves in the reference room. Knowledge of search system commands is not enough to be a good searcher. The real test comes in applying search system knowledge to the subject content of the individual files. The importance of knowing the intricacies of the databases one searches cannot be overstressed.

Costs

Costs for online searching fall into several categories. First there are equipment and software costs. A microcomputer that is set up for online searching can cost anywhere from $1,500 to $4,000 depending upon make, model, and discounts available. Software costs can range from nothing at all to approximately $1,000. If all one intends to do is search, download, and print, there are several good-quality communications packages (such as PC-Talk and PC-Dial) that are either in the public domain or available as shareware that can be acquired at minimal cost. If, however, one wishes to go the route of custom bibliography production and creation of in-house databases from the downloaded material, software expense in the order of $500 to $1,000 is quite standard.

Next are costs that are associated with sign-up or membership, training, and documentation. Some services have an initial sign-up fee, others do not. Generally the sign-up fee is not more than from $50 to $75. Services that have training programs generally charge in the order of $150 for a day-long training session. System documentation may be included in the sign-up fee; otherwise, one can generally expect to spend somewhere between $50 and $75 for system manuals and specific file information.

The next major cost category is the expense related to the actual searching time. Fee schedules and methods of charging vary from vendor to vendor, but generally are linked to the amount of time spent online or the amount of information displayed to the searcher. Traditionally vendors have charged different rates for the different databases they carry, ranging from a low of approximately $25 per hour to a high in the area of $250 per hour. In addition to the connect time charges, some files have charges for the number of records printed, displayed, or downloaded. Usually the cost ranges from $.10 to $.75 per record. Beyond the database use charges there is generally a charge for using the telecommunications network that varies from $6 to $15 per hour depending upon the vendor and network used. Most vendors have some form of discount rates for high-volume users, and group rates for local networks or consortia that contract for a certain minimum amount of use.

Additional costs will come from promotion efforts, continuing education for staff (keeping search skills and knowledge up to date), and supplies such as paper, ribbons, and floppy disks. Staff time is required to conduct searches and for search preparation. Beyond this time there is also additional time required for record keeping. Introduction of online services usually brings about a noticeable increase in interlibrary loan and photocopy requests, which will also require added staff time.

Online searching is expensive, but it provides libraries and other institutions with extremely powerful information retrieval capabilities that, as recently as the 1960s, were considered impossible for any but the largest and most highly funded organizations.

Online Developments of the 1980s

Since its public introduction in the early 1970s, online searching has been an area of rapid change and development: new vendors, new databases, new computer technology, and new search system features and capabilities. The 1980s continued the record of change and development with (1) the commercial introduction of mass data storage using inexpensive CD-ROM devices; (2) the increasing availability of fulltext databases; (3) the introduction of gateway and front-end systems that simplify the searching process and make possible what has been termed end user searching (searching performed by the person who needs the information, rather than by a trained search intermediary); and (4) the increasing appearance of large in-house databases. This section will look at each of these developments in turn.

CD-ROM stands for compact disk–read-only memory. CD-ROM is a form of laser disk, 4.75 inches in diameter, that holds roughly 600,000,000 characters (more than the entire *Encyclopaedia Britannica*). The disk itself is sturdy and plastic coated so that no special handling or care is required. The information is stored on the disk by a high-powered laser that burns a series of microscopic pits into the surface of the disk. The disk is "read" by a CD-ROM reader (cost in 1989 was approximately $700) that is linked to a standard microcomputer. The reader contains a laser whose light is directed onto the surface of the CD-ROM disk. The pits and flat areas of the disk's surface reflect the laser's light differently. These two different reflections represent the binary 1 and 0 of digital information storage. Once mastered the disk cannot be changed, hence the term ROM for read-only memory. While the master or original disk is expensive, the subsequent copies are relatively inexpensive to produce ($10–$20). This means that if there is a large market for a particular database a CD-ROM version can be marketed at a very reasonable price.

The major appeal of CD-ROM is that it brings information back within the local setting, rather than on the computer of a remote vendor, and thereby removes the online connect time expense. Supporting online searching in the 1970s required large mainframe computers with high-capacity disk drives attached. The cost was tremendous, and could not be borne by a single site. Fifteen years has seen tremendous advances in computer technology, to the point where a microcomputer can run sophisticated search software, and entire databases can be stored on CD-ROMs at reasonable cost. Libraries can subscribe to CD-ROM databases in much the same way that they have always subscribed to printed information sources. The locally held CD-ROM database can then be searched as much as desired without concern for online connect charges. One drawback of CD-ROM is that since it cannot be altered or updated the user gives up access to the most current information. Disks are usually updated on a quarterly or monthly basis, so that for access to very recent materials, it is still necessary to use the database of the remote online vendor.

The role that the traditional vendors of mainframe-based online services will take with regard to CD-ROM is not certain. Wilson has released a CD-ROM version of the WILSONLINE search system and databases. DIALOG has released a CD-ROM version of the ERIC database. Some database producers are planning to market their databases directly along with third-party search software. This could greatly increase the number of search systems that searchers would need to know. Many searchers therefore hope that the traditional online vendors can make arrangements with database producers, so that the vendors can market CD-ROM versions of databases bundled together with the same search software that searchers are already accustomed to using. CD-ROM will certainly change the online industry; the specific outcomes, however, are still unfolding.

Another significant development of the 1980s has been the increasing number of fulltext databases available. Early databases were primarily bibliographic, containing citations to the desired information rather than the information itself. A fulltext database, on the other hand, contains the entire text of materials. There are fulltext files of journal articles, newspaper articles, reference books, directories, handbooks, encyclopedias, and textbooks. With fulltext files one can search for specific facts within the text, and also have the complete text available for display or printing while online with no delay.

Searching fulltext files is somewhat different than searching bibliographic files. In fulltext files searchers are advised not to use the straight Boolean AND, because it results in too many false drops. With AND one term can be at the start of the document, and the other term at the end of the document, and the terms can have no relationship to each other at all. Generally searchers are advised to use what are called proximity operators when searching fulltext. Proximity operators vary from system to system, but typically require that words be within so many words of each other, or in the same sentence, or in the same paragraph. Requiring the words to be closer together gives a better chance that they will bear the desired subject relationship. Display options that permit direct viewing of the sections of text where the search match occurred help searchers focus quickly on the information sought. The increasing number of fulltext files gives a clear indication of a growing tendency to use computer technology for a comprehensive approach to information storage and access.

The 1980s also brought about increased activities aimed at making searching more attractive to the end user, the person who needs the information. The introductions of front-end software and gateway systems were major efforts toward that end.

Front-end software operates as a "friendly translator" between the user and the host system. Front ends are generally considered as aids to the novice or less experienced searcher who is not thoroughly familiar with the command language of a host system. Usually front ends function by replacing system commands with a series of fairly simple menu choices. The user conducts a search by selecting appropriate menu choices, and the front-end software then translates the selected menu options into the correct system commands. Some front-end software is designed to work with only one host system (DIALOG'S DIAL-LINK and WILSONLINE'S WILSEARCH); other front-end software supports simplified searching of several host systems (Pro-Search supports DIALOG and BRS; Sci-Mate supports DIALOG, BRS, SDC, Questel, and NLM). Though front-end software removes some of the power and interactive flexibility of online searching, it can be a real help for novice searchers needing to do sample searches.

Gateway systems permit users to connect to a variety of host systems (though only one at a time) without concern for various specific log-on and network procedures. Some gateway systems handle all billing procedures themselves, so a user would not receive separate bills from various host systems (such as BRS, DIALOG, and SDC), but only one bill from the gateway service. It is also quite common for gateway systems to include front-end software that simplifies the search procedures for the various host systems to which they provide access. From the user's point of view, gateway systems generally function like front-end systems, by providing the user with a menu of options from which to select the desired action. The system will then translate the choices into the correct system command statements.

An example of a major gateway system in the United States is Easynet. To use Easynet the user calls a toll-free number (no contract or previous contact is necessary, and charges can be billed to credit cards), and then answers a series of questions aimed at search strategy development. Easynet then automatically connects the user with one of over 700 databases that are available through 13 vendors to which Easynet provides access. Besides simplifying the search process for the novice user, services such as Easynet can help some libraries to offer end user searching through the provision of the direct credit card billing option.

In-house databases are another development that have had a tremendous increase of activity during the 1980s. As the cost of computer storage comes down, and the capability of small computers to run sophisticated search software packages increases, more and more organizations are opting to build and maintain in-house files. How the files are created varies with the particular situation. Depending on the nature of the information to be stored, it may be keyed in directly or downloaded from other existing files (copyright must be taken into account in any downloading procedures).

In-house databases involve two major components: search software to enable access to the information, and storage devices to hold the information. The cost of good database search software continues to decrease. There are several packages available for small computers, among them BRS Search, CAIRS, IN-MAGIC, Pro-Cite, and Sci-Mate. The primary storage device through the 1980s continued to be the hard disk. The "write once read many" (WORM) optical disk (with storage capacity similar to CD-ROM disks) may be a viable option in the future. Data can be written on a WORM optical disk once, and after that it can only be read. This writing is done in house and does not correspond to the first mastering process with CD-ROM. To update the file a new WORM disk would have to be created that included the updated material. Eventually read-

and-write optical disks should become available, which will bring tremendous possibilities and flexibility to in-house database creation and maintenance.

Further Reading

Fenichel, Carol H. *Online Searching: A Primer.* 2nd ed. Medford, N.J.: Learned Information, 1984. An excellent introduction to the various aspects of online searching and also contains a very good list of references and further readings presented by chapter subject areas.

Online: The Magazine of Online Information Systems. Published by Online Inc., 11 Tannery Lane, Weston, Conn. 06883.

"Online Databases." *Library Journal.* Monthly column.

Two highly recommended sources for keeping up to date. *Online* is an excellent practical publication that presents a full range of recent online issues and developments. The Online Databases column in *Library Journal* deals with some of the newest online developments and points to new trends and issues.

While there are numerous other sources available (lists are contained in Fenichel's book) these recommendations are a good starting point both for acquiring more background information on online searching and perhaps more importantly for keeping up with new developments.

Appendix: Major U.S. Vendors of Online Services

Bibliographic Retrieval Services, Inc. (BRS)
1200 Route 7
Latham, New York 12110

Compuserve, Inc.
5000 Arlington Center Boulevard
P.O. Box 20212
Columbus, Ohio 43220

DIALOG Information Services, Inc.
3460 Hillview Avenue
Palo Alto, California 94304

Dow Jones and Company, Inc.
P.O. Box 300
Princeton, New Jersey 08540

Mead Data Central (MDC)
933 Springboro Pike
Dayton, Ohio 45401

National Library of Medicine (NLM)
8600 Rockville Pike
Bethesda, Maryland 20209

SDC Information Services
2500 Colorado Avenue
Santa Monica, California 90406

The Source
Source Telecomputing
Company
1616 Anderson Road
McLean, Virginia 22102

Wilsonline
H. W. Wilson Company
950 University Avenue
Bronx, New York 10452

PART

3

The Practice of Information Science in Library Organizations

CHAPTER

7

Organizations and Information Systems

Michael G. Bowen
Patricia Bick

One way to assess the effectiveness of organizations is to focus on their capabilities to collect, interpret, order, manipulate, produce, and disseminate information.[1] The commonsense notion implicit in analyzing organizations in this way is that enterprises that do a better job of "information management" should be more effective than those that are less adept as information managers. The truth, insofar as there are any truths about organizations or their analysis, is that this view is overly simple. This is because, in this case, "common sense" makes a number of assumptions about the direct causal relationship between information and organizational effectiveness that might not be appropriate. Since this issue of causality is so critical to justifications of information use and information systems design and development in organizations, an evaluation of this presumed causal connection between information and effectiveness is necessary.

The purpose of this chapter, therefore, is to discuss the role of information and information systems management as they might influence the overall effectiveness of organizations. To do this, a brief review of the types of decisions that have to be made in organizational settings, and an analysis of the "information" that is used to make decisions, will be presented. From these, discussion of a general model of decision making in organizations can proceed: a model that will allow some insight into the relationship between information and effectiveness as an outcome of managerial decision making.

Types of Organizational Decisions

It is commonly believed that decision making in organizations can be classified along the lines of three theoretical levels of management: (1) strategic; (2) managerial; and (3) operational. Each of these hierarchical levels is therefore understood as presenting a particular type of decision to those in authority, decisions which collectively define and maintain the activities (and individuals) that distinguish one organization from another. These three theoretically distinct levels of managerial responsibility will be considered individually.

---

1. The term "information" is defined as any physical form of representation, or surrogate, of knowledge or of a particular thought, used for communication. See J. Farradane, "The Nature of Information," *Journal of Information Science* 1:13–17 (1979).

Strategic

Decision making at the strategic level is the primary responsibility of the upper echelon of any organization's management. Here, top managers must make the decisions that establish the parameters that define in what areas the organization will conduct its activities. These decisions thus define the "business" or "mission" of the organization. Operationally, these decisions often involve difficult choices, including: (1) the objectives of the organization; (2) the resources to be used to achieve the objectives; and (3) the strategies, policies, and criteria that determine the acquisition, use, and disposition of those resources. Decisions at the strategic level of management, therefore, involve the formulation of long-range strategies, plans, objectives, and policies for an organization.

Managerial

Decision making at the managerial level is the primary responsibility of those individuals or groups charged with the administration of the so-called functional areas of management. Staff functions, such as accounting, marketing, and finance in business organizations, and acquisitions, personnel, and cataloging in library organizations, fall within the purview of this level of management. Decisions at this level, therefore, direct the processes that ensure that resources are obtained and reallocated efficiently in the accomplishment of the organization's objectives.

Operational

Decision making at the level of operations is the primary responsibility of those managers having "line" authority within an organization; that is, it involves those managers who directly control the activities that produce the product or service of an enterprise. Reference services, periodicals/serials, circulation, and interlibrary loan services in libraries might serve as examples of functions at this level of management. Managerial control within these functions is thus to ensure that production tasks are carried out efficiently.

As can be seen in the above descriptions, strategies within each of the levels of management are based upon their own unique sets of issues and challenges. Beyond the content of these strategies, however, lies a fundamental distinction in the manner in which these decisions can be made. This distinction is mainly, yet debatably, between the "strategic" and "managerial and operational" levels of decision making and involves the relative abilities of decision makers to "structure" the decision situations in question.

Ill-structured versus Well-structured Problems

The ability to "structure" or organize a problem situation so that it can be more easily solved is generally considered to be relative to the power (and patience) of the problem solver's, or problem-solving system's, decision-making techniques.[2]

2. H. A. Simon, "The Structure of Ill-Structured Problems," *Artificial Intelligence* 4:181–201 (1973).

Although problem-solving techniques are always limited in their ability to produce a "correct" solution by the uncertainty of the future, some situations can be structured to a far greater degree than can others. Quite simply, the future is more knowable or predictable in some cases than it is in others. Decision scientists have described these different kinds of situations as belonging somewhere along a continuum, the opposing ends of which have been labeled "well-structured" and "ill-structured." It will be useful to outline the conceptual distinctions between these two classifications.

"Well-structured" decision situations are those in which the decision criteria, mechanisms for achieving a solution, and desired outcomes are well-specified, complete, and familiar to a problem solver.[3] One simple example of a well-structured decision situation is represented by the equation $X + 2 = 4$. The decision-making situation (i.e., the context in which you need to know the correct value of X) and problem (i.e., the equation to be solved) can be considered to be well-structured because the decision criteria (i.e., both sides of the equation, which consist of known and understood variables or quantities, must equal 4), the mechanism for achieving a solution (i.e., subtract 2 from each side of the equation), and the desired outcome (i.e., the solution for X that makes both sides of the equation equal, in this case 2) indeed meet the above criteria for these particular problem solvers (the authors).

On the other hand, "ill-structured" decision situations exist in cases where the above criteria cannot be met. In other words, ill-structured problems occur as: (1) there is ambiguity and incompleteness of the problem-related information; (2) problems are continually defined and redefined by managers; (3) there is the lack of a program for the desired outcomes; (4) multiperson influence becomes a possibility; and (5) decisions are made over an extended period of time.[4] A question such as "Should our library collect microcomputer software for the use of our patrons?" represents such a problem in a library context.

At the present time, most, if not all, organization scholars would agree that strategic problems are "ill-structured."[5] The reason for this belief is that, since

3. K. R. MacCrimmon and R. N. Taylor, "Decision Making and Problem Solving," in M. D. Dunnette, ed., *Handbook of Industrial and Organizational Psychology* (Chicago: Rand McNally, 1976), 1397–1453; D. Gerwin and F. D. Tuggle, "Modeling Organizational Decisions Using the Human Problem Solving Paradigm," *Academy of Management Review* 3:762–773 (1978).

4. G. R. Ungson, D. N. Braunstein, and P. D. Hall, "Managerial Information Processing: A Research Review," *Administrative Science Quarterly* 26:116–134 (1981).

5. J. M. Beyer, "Ideologies, Values, and Decision Making in Organizations," in P. C. Nystrom and W. H. Starbuck, eds., *Handbook of Organizational Design*, vol. 2 (New York: Oxford University Press, 1981), 166–202; H. A. Simon, *Administrative Behavior* (New York: Macmillan, 1945); H. A. Simon, *Models of Man* (New York: John Wiley & Sons, 1957); Simon, "The Structure of Ill-Structured Problems," 181–201; A. Newell, "Heuristic Programming: Ill-Structured Problems," in J. Aronofsky, ed., *Progress in Operations Research*, vol. 3 (New York: John Wiley & Sons, 1969); H. Mintzberg, D. Raisinghani, and A. Theoret, "The Structure of 'Unstructured' Decision Processes," *Administrative Science Quarterly* 27:548–570 (1976); M. D. Davis, *Game Theory* (New York: Basic Books, 1970); J. D. Thompson and A. Tuden, "Strategies, Structures and Processes of Organizational Decision," in J. D. Thompson and others, eds., *Comparative Studies in Administration* (Pittsburgh: The University of Pittsburgh Press, 1959); G. Vickers, *The Art of Judgment: A Study of Policy Making* (New York: Basic Books, 1965).

strategic problems do not meet the above criteria, there is simply no way to decide whether such decisions are acceptable before receiving feedback on the outcome of an already implemented strategy. There are, however, many decisions at the managerial and operational levels of organization for which one can decide whether a strategy (i.e., a decision) is acceptable before it is implemented. These well-structured, or at least potentially structurable, decision situations can be found in repetitive or routine contexts where the situation remains (or is assumed to be) so stable that it need not be completely reanalyzed for every decision. This kind of decision making is often formalized through the use of management information systems (MIS) at the operating level, and electronic data systems (EDS) at the managerial level.

The ill-structured decision situations found at the strategic level of management are more controversial in this regard, however, because of a lack of consensus about the current and ultimate limitations of decision science techniques to structure such situations. Some, for example, believe that the development of decision support systems (DSS) in organizations can prove invaluable when confronting ill-structured problems. These systems attempt to structure ill-structured problems through the use of computer simulation models, models that allow preimplementation testing and analysis of strategies developed from different sets of assumptions or combinations of variables. Proponents feel that as DSS are developed and better understood, these support systems will provide top-level managements with sharper insights into the consequences of hypothetical strategy proposals.

Despite this argument, however, others would not accept such an optimistic view of the potential of such systems. Their belief is that since the future is unpredictable, efforts to quantify that uncertainty can be dangerously misleading, if not erroneous. This is not only because of the nature of the "unquantifiable" assumptions which require quantification by these techniques, but also by the fact that important variables may be either unknown or omitted in any analysis. Interestingly though, not a part of this public discussion is the idea that management intuition and experience, rather than a programmable approach, must serve as the primary architect of any strategy proposal. There would thus seem to be some general agreement that only the mind of a decision maker can create form and substance from an ill-structured issue.[6] Once this initial framework has been developed, however, the use of decision-making aids such as DSS can prove to be quite valuable.

Decision Making in Organizations Reconsidered

Several factors complicate the rather neatly segmented theoretical framework for the content and process of managerial decision making outlined above. The first "complication" is that managers within each of the three levels must make

6. J. D. Morecroft, "Strategy Support Models," *Strategic Management Journal* 5:215–229 (1984).

decisions that have the characteristics of decision making within all three levels of management. That is, managers throughout an organization make many decisions that are potentially well structured, as well as those that are inherently ill structured. For example, the strategic level of management is usually thought of as involving the development of long-range strategies, plans, goals, and policies for an organization. In practice, however, top management must also ensure that adequate resources are allocated and then efficiently employed in the administration and development of strategies, as well as assure that these processes are proceeding effectively. In other words, top-level executives must make decisions that present the same types of structurable problems as those ordinarily considered to be the sole responsibility of the managerial and operational levels of management.

Similarly, decision makers within the managerial level of an organization must establish the long-range strategies, plans, goals, and policies of their respective functional areas (strategic types), and assure that those under their supervision carry out their responsibilities efficiently (operational types). Just as at the strategic level, there are both structurable and unstructurable problems at this level of management. In addition, decision making at the operational level of management must also consider strategic and managerial decision types in the normal course of events—decision situations that involve the strategic planning for, acquisition of, and efficient use of resources under their control.

Managers at all levels of an organization face a full array of decision types and problems. There are problems at each level which have at least the potential to be routinely structured or formalized as learning occurs, and those which do not (situations that are so new that learning from past decision making is of little current use). Figure 7.1 shows these general relationships between managerial level, decision content, and decision type. Figure 7.1 also specifically addresses these relationships in library organizations by suggesting examples of the kinds of decisions at each level.[7]

Another complication relates to the size and internal structuring of organizations, as the degree of differentiation and specialization of tasks will often differ widely depending upon those factors. For example, in organizations having only one or two layers of management, such as a small public, branch, or special library, the distinction between strategic, managerial, and operational levels of management does not exist. One person, the library director, usually makes all three types of decisions. In contrast, within organizations where there are several layers of management, such as can be found in a large company like the General Motors Corporation or some major university research libraries, tasks and decision-making authority are differentiated and distributed to specialists. In such

7. A library organization is a very special type of organization. Unlike the larger organizations of which they are most often a part (e.g., a university; business organization; city, state, or federal government), they do not ordinarily generate operating revenues. For the most part, a library's resources are obtained from allocations from the larger organization, allocations which are justifiable for that organization because the library's services are felt to be important. The implications of this to library management are important in that in all but the very largest and most complex libraries the preponderance of managerial activities and decision making are at the operating level.

Level of Management	Decision Content	Library Example	Decision Type
Strategic/Top Organizational level responsibility: Long-range plans, policies, missions, objectives	Strategic—establish long-range plans and goals of planning process	Plan for planning	Unstructurable
	Managerial—efficiently obtain and allocate resources for planning process	Assign responsibilities, allocate funds, space	Structurable
	Operational—assure effective planning process	Provide deadlines, enforce deadlines, rewards for timeliness	Structurable
Managerial/Middle Organizational level responsibility: Obtain and allocate resources efficiently	Strategic—establish divisional long-range plans, policies, goals	Establish processes and policies of automation/technical services	Unstructurable
	Managerial—efficiently obtain and allocate resources within a division	Obtain additional staff, allocate funds for retrospective conversion	Structurable
	Operational—assure divisional tasks and supervision are carried out efficiently	Assure proper training of staff for efficiency	Structurable
Operational/Line Organizational level responsibility: Assure production tasks are carried out efficiently	Strategic—establish production planning process and policies	Establish process and policies by which quotas for retrospective conversion will be set	Unstructurable
	Managerial—efficiently obtain and allocate resources for production responsibilities	Determine and acquire staffing and equipment needs	Structurable
	Operational—assure production supervision and tasks are carried out efficiently	Control activities and monitor reports as to quality of work completed	Structurable

Figure 7.1. Managerial decision making

companies, managerial levels are thus far more distinct, despite the fact that decision-making input often transcends managerial level in many companies. For instance, operational-level managers may have input into the decisions made at the managerial and strategic levels, but not decision-making authority, as an important part of a company's strategic planning process.

A third complicating factor is the number, completeness, strength, and enforcement of formal or informal policies and procedures: that is, the extent that work is formally structured. The fewer, less complete, and less strict are organizational rules, standard operating procedures, institutional norms, and so on, the greater the latitude that individuals have to make the decisions which control their own work. Since no organization can completely structure its employees' activities, it is usually assumed that some of this "unmanaged" decision making always occurs. One implication of this is that what are often viewed as "organizational activities" are not always the result of institutionally sanctioned managerial decisions.

Two additional complications deserve mention here. One is that the above framework does not account for the observation that decision makers "enact" the reality that they interpret as information. The other complication, related to this point, is the recognition that these enactments are essentially "myths," which are often subject to negotiations, distortion, and political wrangling. These require explanation.

Information and Myths as Enactments in Organizations

If one believes that organizations doing a better job of information management are or will be more effective than those less adept as information managers, then one is making some far-reaching assumptions about the directional causal relationships between "information," the decisions that are based upon that information, and the effectiveness of those decisions as measured by the observed outcomes. Among these are:

1. "Information" exists in an objective sense. It is therefore possible to identify and collect "the" information necessary for proper decision making.
2. "Objective" weightings or valuations of "the" information exist. The "best" way of understanding information can be used to identify "the" problem and "the" solution to the problem. The "solution," of course, represents the optimal strategy or decision given the objectively defined situation.
3. There is a direct causal link between the choice of strategy and the outcome of the decision. In other words, if one chooses "the proper" strategy, the desired outcome (which signifies effectiveness) will be achieved.
4. An objective measure of "the" desired outcome, and thus an objective measure of effectiveness, exists.

If viewed in light of the earlier discussion of well- and ill-structured decision situations, these assumptions seem reasonable only to the extent that a particular problem is structurable. Problems are structurable, however, only to the extent that the decision maker's experience, prior learning, and knowledge lead to a way of allowing a useful prediction of the future to be made, "useful" in the sense that one can predict the outcome of the strategy, implied by a decision, with a proven or acceptable degree of accuracy. A simple library-related example of such a structurable situation would be that if experience has shown that there is no demand for professional reference services during certain times of the day, week, month, or academic year, then it would be best not to go to the expense of providing reference services during those particular times.

Problems that are essentially unstructurable, where "useful" predictions of the future are far more problematic, render the above assumptions unreasonable. Reality, or the information upon which a decision is based, is in part created by decision makers, and the nature of those constructions is that multiple alternative interpretations of circumstances and events are always legitimate and often the rule. One excellent example of such an unstructurable problem was the undeclared war in Vietnam. Because alternative interpretations of the circumstances surrounding the decisions which led first to our country's escalating involvement in and then withdrawal from the war effort were so fundamental and heartfelt, the debate over the issues continues even today. What, for example, should the policy makers in the government have done differently to bring victory? Did we have sufficient cause to enter the Vietnam conflict in the first place? By not giving a total military effort to the war, which resulted in our losing the war, did we disgrace the memories of those soldiers who died or were disabled there? Should we have pulled our forces from Vietnam years earlier than we did because a military solution to that deeply rooted conflict was impossible; because it was clear very early in our involvement that we could never win such a war; or, more basically, because the war was immoral?

Another example of an unstructurable problem is inherent in the different points of view often held by individuals performing "technical services" and those performing "public services" in libraries. The technical services function, on the one hand, is concerned with the efficiency of acquiring and cataloging materials, whereas the public services area is concerned with the convenience of and service to library patrons. To what extent should concerns for operational efficiency override concerns for services to patrons, or vice versa?

Critical to our understanding of the legitimacy of opposing points of view, such as those represented in the above examples, is some perspective on the "information" that each point of view is based upon. To accomplish this understanding we need to focus directly on the development of "points of view" in organizations and the information used in this development. Hedberg's model of organizations as learning systems offers some initial direction in this effort.[8]

8. B. Hedberg, "How Organizations Learn and Unlearn," in *Handbook of Organizational Design*, vol. 1, 3–27.

Organizations as Learning Systems

In essence, the argument presented thus far in this chapter is that if information is to be of any help in generating organizational actions, it must either: (1) be useful within the context of a well-structured or routinized decision situation; or (2) contribute to the development of a point of view from which a judgment can be made in ill-structured or non-routinized decision situations. The reader should note that in both of the above instances, a point of view (i.e., a theory of causal relationships, and therefore, action) that gives structure to the decision maker's perception of reality and thus focuses decision making is the central feature. According to Hedberg, these theories of action are appropriately called "myths" because that word emphasizes the multiple origins that these theories might have. For example, myths are developed at times from observation or experience, at times from the input of others, and at times from sheer fantasy. Just as the ancient Greeks and Romans created their elaborate mythologies to help them understand and act "effectively" in their world, we construct theories so that we can function more effectively (i.e., create useful understandings and subsequent predictions as bases for action) in our world.

Hedberg's concept of organizational myths is consistent with the rather extensive, and growing, psychological literature dealing with the creation of theories or models of causal influence (causal modeling) by individuals attempting to structure the situations in which they find themselves.[9] Hedberg's model also has close ties to the organizational behavior literature that emphasizes the importance of power and sociopolitical influence to decision making.[10] According to Hedberg, myths are thus integral frameworks for decision making, and sources of conflict, within organizations.

Figure 7.2 suggests the logic of Hedberg's model: myths, which evolve from partial mappings of past realities, are theories that generate strategies and, subsequently, actions. Strategies are thus hypotheses (essentially guesses) and actions (interactions with reality) that ultimately verify or falsify the underlying theory. It is important to emphasize that myths are "constructed" from the information that is perceived.[11] In a strict sense, however, it may be more correct to say that myths are based upon "enacted" information, or more simply, "enactments."

9. R. P. Abelson, "Script Processing in Attitude Formation and Decision Making," in J. S. Carroll and J. W. Payne, eds., *Cognition and Social Behavior* (Hillsdale, N.J.: Lawrence Erlbaum, 1976), 33–45; C. Argyris and D. A. Schon, *Organizational Learning* (Reading, Mass.: Addison-Wesley, 1978); H. J. Einhorn and R. M. Hogarth, "Prediction, Diagnosis, and Causal Thinking in Forecasting," *Journal of Forecasting* 1:23–26 (1982).

10. M. D. Cohen, J. G. March, and J. P. Olsen, "A Garbage Can Model of Organizational Choice," *Administrative Science Quarterly* 17:1–25 (1972); R. M. Cyert and J. G. March, *A Behavioral Theory of the Firm* (Englewood Cliffs, N.J.: Prentice-Hall, 1963); A. M. Pettigrew, *The Politics of Organizational Decision Making* (London: Tavistock, 1973); J. Pfeffer and G. R. Salancik, *The External Control of Organizations* (New York: Harper & Row, 1978).

11. This is meant in the large sense of the word "information," where even fantasy can be considered information.

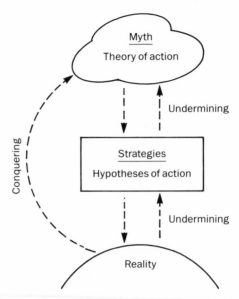

Source: B. Hedberg, "How Organizations Learn and Grow." in Nystrom and Starbuck, eds., *Handbook of Organizational Design* (Oxford and New York: Oxford University Press, 1981) vol. 1, p. 12.

Figure 7.2. Illustration of Hedberg's model

Enactments in Organizations

The noted scholar Karl Weick has most eloquently argued the case for enactment. In his book *The Social Psychology of Organizing,* Weick suggests that the term "enactment" is useful in describing human perception in information gathering because it focuses directly on the important role that people play in creating the environments that affect them.[12] In practice, the concept "enactment" can be understood as describing the ways that we come to develop our theories of the world around us, explicitly considering our individual or collective parts in the construction of those myths. Some examples of enactments will help to show how this concept describes an integral part of our everyday sense making. The first two examples appeared in other sources; the authors prepared the third enactment.

> Imagine that the major input to be processed by employees is either a stock market tickertape with no spaces between symbols, or a teletype machine whose output contains no punctuation into sentences or paragraphs. In the unpunctuated output one does not know where one "story" leaves off and another story begins, or even whether a story is a reasonable unit of analysis. The same thing is true in the case of the unpunctuated stock market tickertape. In both cases there is a mass of data, without any hints concerning their importance. It's the job of the employee to tear off portions

12. K. E. Weick, *The Social Psychology of Organizing* (Reading, Mass.: Addison-Wesley, 1979).

of the tickertape or teletype for further study. Those activities of tearing are crude kinds of enactments. Once something has been isolated, then that is the environment momentarily for the organization, and that environment has been put into place by the very actions of the employees themselves.[13]

Cooperators and competitors develop different views of what other people are like. And in the case of competitors, their presumption that other individuals are universally competitive leads them to act in such a manner that they produce, in cooperative individuals, that competitiveness that they assume was there all along. The competitive players simply don't see cooperative overtures in the beginning. Instead they act in such a way that the cooperative players modify their efforts and become competitive, thereby fulfilling the original competitors' definition that all people are competitive.[14]

Despite hard economic times, library managers have been buying more costly computer systems in order to save labor and at the same time provide patrons with a higher quantity and quality of services. But with this new technology has come problems. Libraries now need highly trained technicians to operate, maintain, and update the computers and computing services; some of the more traditionally minded employees have been alienated by the new technology; and the expensive system may require higher usage rates to be cost effective. The result of all of this has been to necessitate larger budget allocations, not only to maintain the upgraded quality and quantity of services, but also to fund the additional services made possible by the automation. In the absence of sufficiently larger budget allocations, however, some heretofore essential services, personnel, and so on, not connected with the large capital outlays for the now necessary machines, have had to suffer reductions.

If, as both Hedberg and Weick would argue, myths in organizations are based upon the information produced by individual or group enactments, it becomes clear that the different points of view in ill-structured decision contexts are not truths or objectively understood issues but represent alternative enactments of a situation. The model represented in Figure 7.3 addresses this idea in detail by arguing that because they are subjectively enacted and either implicitly or explicitly considered, myths, problem definition, strategies, implementation of the chosen strategy, and outcomes are all arguable in strategic decision-making situations throughout an organization. Specifically, the model suggests that a number of interacting alternative myths may exist within an organization that are potential competitors for control of the organization's strategic agenda. From each of these myths, alternative and possibly competing definitions of particular problems or issues emerge. It is from these problem definitions that strategies, appropriate to any particular problem definition, are devised. The strategy that achieves dominance, possibly formulated and approved as a compromise with alternative strategies, is then implemented. At this point, as it has been throughout this cycle, data is provided by feedback channels (both formal and informal

13. Ibid., 153–154.
14. Ibid., 164.

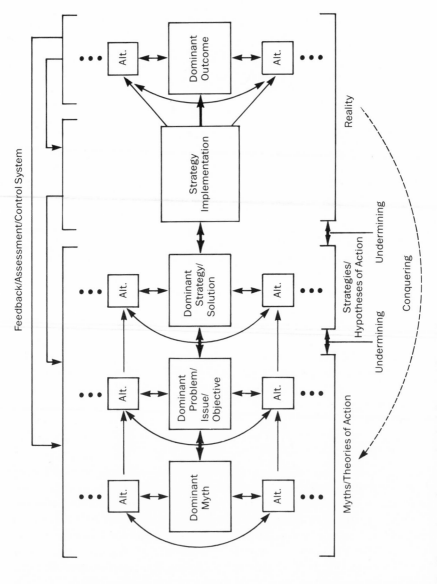

Figure 7.3. Illustration of strategic decision making and outcomes

information systems) for the use in and enactment of outcomes. This feedback allows for the evaluation of the dominant myth, perhaps through its consequences, as the process continues.

The legitimacy and frequency of alternative perspectives in organizations also imply the significance of political activity as an appropriate means of resolving any disagreements among different viewpoints. Political wrangling and maneuvering, often considered to be purposeless or dysfunctional, are thus vital to decision making in organizations as a potential aid in the development (negotiation) of a more balanced viewpoint upon which a decision can be based. In theory, a more balanced, broadly based perspective should allow for the consideration of additional information items that may be important to increasing the organization's chances of success.

This is not to state, however, that there might not be negative aspects to expressly political behavior. For example, Feldman and March, in their review of the research literature on decision making in organizations, noted some potentially dysfunctional consequences of the politics of information and information management in ill-structured situations, and made a number of observations about the gathering and use of information in organizations:

1. Much of the information that is gathered and communicated by individuals in organizations has little decision relevance.
2. Much of the information that is used to justify a decision is collected and interpreted after the decision has been made, or substantially made.
3. Much of the information gathered in response to requests for information is not considered in the making of decisions for which it is requested.
4. Regardless of the information available at the time a decision is considered, more information is requested.
5. Complaints that an organization does not have enough information to make a decision occur while available information is ignored.
6. The relevance of the information to the decision being made is less conspicuous than is the insistence on information.
7. Information is subject to misrepresentation in organizations; it can be gathered and communicated in a context of conflict of interest and with consciousness of potential decision consequences.[15]

From the "classical" decision theory point of view, information is gathered because it helps a decision maker to make a decision: it is acquired to the point where the marginal expected costs of that information equal the marginal expected return from that information. As Feldman and March have concluded, however, observations of decision making in organizations are not easy to reconcile with this view. Seemingly, investments in information are often made with apparently little regard for the principles of decision theory. "Organizational participants seem to find value in information that has no great

15. M. S. Feldman and J. G. March, "Information in Organizations as Signal and Symbol," *Administrative Science Quarterly* 26:171–186 (1981).

decision relevance. They gather information and do not use it. They ask for reports and do not read them. They act first and receive requested information later."[16]

One hypothetical example of these points in a university library setting would be the process of allocating funds for book purchases for the various academic units across campus. In accordance with generally accepted ways of structuring such situations, librarians ordinarily collect information such as the number of students majoring in an academic discipline, the number of yearly graduates, terminal degree offered by area of study, and the number of teaching faculty. This information might then be used in the development of a set of decision criteria or for comparison against a set of pre-established decision criteria. The allocation process, however, is awash in political activities resulting from the application of pressure by various interests to influence allocation decisions in the direction of their own priorities. For example, if a certain part of a collection has been identified as being particularly strong, proponents of one point of view might argue that that collection should be allocated whatever funds would be necessary to make it "outstanding." On the other hand, others might argue that the strong areas should be given less funds so that deficient areas might be improved. In addition, the teaching faculty at the university is likely to make certain (sometimes very loudly) that the decision makers know its needs, demands, and expectations so that its point of view is given the highest priority. Under these conditions, it is likely that these political considerations will influence allocation decisions to some degree at the expense of the more objective criteria. Also under these conditions, it is more likely that information can and will be used as a justification for decisions, rather than as the input for decision making.

Information and Effectiveness

We are now in a position to make some rather explicit statements about the relationships between information, information management, and the effectiveness of organizations. The major points brought forward thus far in this chapter are:

1. Decision makers at all levels of an organization's hierarchy make an assortment of ill-structured and well-structured (or at least structurable) decisions. Differences between these decision types reflect the extent to which one can predict the future within the environments in which those decisions are made.

2. Myths, as enacted theories of action, generate strategies that can be thought of as hypotheses or guesses. These hypotheses are tested if and when they are implemented and allowed to interact with the world.

16. Ibid., 182.

3. The validity of personal myths, which provide the basis for decision making, is often argued and perhaps often negotiated by those who would seek to determine the activities, priorities, and so on within an organization.

4. Many decisions in organizations are structured, to varying degrees, by precedent, institutional norms, policies, rules, standard operating procedures, and so on. Many others, however, are not. Some decisions and subsequent actions are therefore not the result of institutionally sanctioned managerial decision making. Also, there is oftentimes little apparent connection between the classical decision theory model and actual decision behavior in ill-structured and some potentially structurable decision situations.

Implied in all of the above are the underpinnings of an understanding of the concept "effectiveness" as applied to organizations. Since this term is an important component of the critical issue being focused upon in this chapter, it is worth briefly discussing "effectiveness" at this point.

If, as Figure 7.3 suggests, organizational outcomes are also enacted, one might expect that any political debate or activity will likely involve attempts to create or negotiate some consensual view of how a strategy has performed. The creation of any outcome is based, however, upon a subjective enactment of the data supplied by formal and informal information sources. As suggested earlier, these enactments thus represent the information that can be compared against any existing criteria for determining the effectiveness of the organization's activities. It is important to remember, however, that by definition, objective, prespecified effectiveness criteria cannot exist in ill-structured decision situations. Even though there may be predominant criteria that have developed over time to add structure to similar situations, the point is that alternative criteria are not only possible but are also legitimate. This suggests that, in any particular case, the meaning of "organizational effectiveness" is itself an enactment.

The management literature currently stresses the subjectivity of the criteria upon which measures of "organizational effectiveness" are based. Consistent with the above discussion, the predominant view is that many alternative measures of effectiveness might be utilized to assess an organization's activities. This uncertainty creates dilemmas for managers trying to decide which criteria to meet, thus necessitating decisions dealing with difficult issues such as what to do, how to manage, what constituencies to satisfy, who to offend, and so on.[17] Even the more popularized, yet comparable, term "excellence" is subject to the same controversies about the nature of effective action.[18] What apparently seem like effective actions to some, certainly do not seem so to others holding different assessment criteria.

17. K. Cameron and D. W. Whetten, *Organizational Effectiveness: A Comparison of Multiple Models* (New York: Academic Press, 1983); A. Van De Ven and D. L. Ferry, *Measuring and Assessing Organizations* (New York: John Wiley & Sons, 1980); R. F. Zammuto, *Assessing Organizational Effectiveness* (Albany: State University of New York Press, 1982).

18. "Who's Excellent Now?" *Business Week,* 5 November 1984, 76–88; T. J. Peters and R. H. Waterman, *In Search of Excellence* (New York: Warner Books, 1982).

The lesson that we might abstract from the above discussion is that, even disregarding cases in which outcomes produced by factors outside of the organization's control (including pure dumb luck) influence impressions of whether an action was effective or not, there is no necessary causal connection between information systems management, its subsequent effects on decision making, and organizational effectiveness. On the other hand, in many instances there can be and often is.

Earlier in this chapter, we suggested the types of decisions that are at least potentially well-structured (i.e., managerial and operational types of decisions) and those that are more likely to be ill-structured (i.e., strategic decision types) at any level of an organization. It seems logical then that the more structurable the problem, the greater the causal connection between effective information systems management and pre-implementation organizational effectiveness *measures*. It is therefore in these cases that information systems play an important, yet understandably limited, role in the overall effective operation and maintenance of an organization. Contrary, however, to the impression that this statement might give, information systems (both formal and informal) do serve a crucial purpose in strategic decision making. They provide the basis for the enactments which represent the alternative perspectives that are so often important to the generation of a more balanced viewpoint in ill-structured decision situations. Such balanced viewpoints should, as suggested earlier, help to increase the organization's chances of developing a political consensus (if necessary) around the creation and development over time of sensible effectiveness criteria, the development of commitment to the strategies formulated to meet those criteria (or, in the absence of criteria), and thus the assessment of the outcomes of those strategies. In this way, an organization increases its chances to achieve its vision of success.

Summary

The purpose of this chapter was to discuss the role of information and information systems as they might influence overall organizational effectiveness. The result of this discussion has been to place these constructs into the dynamic and often very subjective context of decision making in organizations, a context where enacted information is the driving force behind strategy formulation and implementation but is not the only relevant factor. Forces outside of the control of decision makers at any managerial level of an organization, including luck, are also powerful determinants of whether a favorable or unfavorable comparison will be made between enacted outcomes and enacted effectiveness measures. The role of information systems management is nonetheless crucial because effective policy making and learning may be possible, in the long run, only if the information used in decision making allows for a meaningful consideration of both well- and ill-structured issues.

CHAPTER

8

Administering the Library Automation Process

John E. Evans

The automation of library functions and activities is an undeniable reality of library development. From its earliest applications, the advantages of converting routine and repetitive processes to some form of automation were recognized, and such use of automation became a long-term objective of library management. Often short-term realities proved to be imposing, but in recent years successful automation projects have become rather commonplace. What has significantly changed over time is, in part, the vast improvement of equipment, and the concomitant reduction in cost. More importantly, changes in the library profession have emphasized the development of technological competence, the application of systems analysis to the evaluation of procedures, and the integration of work flows. These, coupled with comprehensive planning and professional management, are the foundations of successful library automation.

Economic pressures on libraries have for more than a decade compelled library leadership to recognize that the thought of self-sufficiency of individual libraries was probably never more than a hopelessly ideal goal. Consequently the economies of cooperative collection development, resource sharing, shared access, and networking have encouraged the development of technology-based solutions to traditional problems of information delivery to the user. Automation, which is by no means inexpensive, offers, if not the reality of cost reduction, then the ability to continue or extend services which otherwise would have been completely impossible or severely limited due to intralibrary resource constraints.

Generally speaking, library automation can provide (1) control of incremental per unit and per task cost increases by improving staff work flow productivity; (2) the opportunity for extension of library services beyond the walls of the building; and (3) the concentration of resources in materials and services rather than in overhead and processing costs.

The current impetus toward automation reflects not only a change of attitude on the part of librarians, but also the changes in the financial demands on libraries and the functional capabilities and attributes of the systems themselves. More powerful machines, available at lower per unit and per task costs, have made automation a library reality. The relative success, though, of the project is attributable not to the price, but rather to the professional, technical, and managerial effort exercised in the process.

While the fundamentals of library practice will remain essentially the same, the inherent truth of library automation is that it represents and functions as a significant agent of change. What will remain constant throughout the process is that high-quality management is essential to a successful undertaking. At face value library automation may appear to be principally and profoundly technological in nature. However, observers will argue that over time the profession has witnessed numerous technological advances or other changes. These come and go. What remain and endure are administration, management, and the application of professional skill, knowledge, and perspective in a problem-solving, process-oriented venture.

The key term in all of this activity and throughout this writing is that of "*process.*" *Library automation is not an event; it is a process.* The actual implementation of the system, the installation of the hardware, the loading of the databases, the first booting of the operating system all will come to appear as mere activities that are but small parts of the automating process. What will come to pervade all of these activities is the realization that the conduct of the process is itself the central focus.

As the library approaches the automation project it is important to do so from the perspective of "What can the library provide to its users as a system, a process, and a service in fulfillment of its traditional mission and goals?" Among these one would normally include high-quality information services to the user community and accurate, authoritative records. Furthermore, these traditional goals should never be lost from sight whether the task at hand is system specification, evaluation, or implementation. Library automation must function for the particular library. It is incumbent on the staff and administration to bring into the process all aspects of library operations and to subject them to a rigorous analysis.

Regardless of the initial disposition toward automation activities, it is important to understand that there are advantages and disadvantages to all systems and practices. Library automation as it confronts the library profession currently offers not a panacea to all of the historical problems that have arisen in the practice of librarianship but rather offers the next phase of improvements in library systems, processing, and control. As such it represents a comprehensive, developing alternative to existing systems and services through the application of information storage and retrieval theory and concept into the practice of librarianship. This imposition of theory onto practice is also influenced by library administration and management theory and practice, bringing these conceptual constructs to bear on the systems, practices, procedures, rules, and materials throughout the existing library structure. Automation is not simple and certainly not easy, but in comparison with the alternative, namely, the continuance of historical practices, it has come to be perceived as the preferred order of business. From the outside looking in it is entirely too easy to be unduly daunted by the seeming complexity of the tasks ahead. Failing to acknowledge these complexities is a problem in and of itself, but recent history demonstrates that library automation is not only a do-able process, but more often than not, it is highly successful.

The Characteristics of Library Automation

Library automation owes its extensive influence on the library in part to what it represents and how that influence is made manifest. Among other attributes:

Library automation is diverse and all-encompassing, affecting the entire library organization and all its clientele.

Library automation is profoundly influential on the future course of all library practices.

Library automation calls into service all skills and talents of the staff.

Library automation demands application of the most fundamental principles of library and information science.

Library automation requires the application of all principles of information storage and retrieval to the daily practice of library service.

Library automation causes an intensive and extensive analysis and reevaluation of all aspects of library activity and procedures by the entire staff.

Library automation causes a rewriting of the library's procedures, creating integrated work flows transcending traditional departmental boundaries.

Library automation is a significant and powerful event in the history of the library, necessitating the beginning of a review, analysis, and modification process governing all library activities and practices. Library automation will issue a new order of library operation. This process is, for all practical purposes, endless.

Finally, library automation is essentially a series of compromises that mediates between what is desired and what is possible.

The Objectives of Library Automation

If we accept that the goals of library automation, as presented above, include the provision of improved or extended high-quality information services and accurate and authoritative record keeping, then what objectives must be accomplished in the pursuit of these goals? A basic list might include the following objectives:

1. The first objective is the improved quality of bibliographic records for all library materials. Libraries frequently couple automation database creation with retrospective conversion (RECON) of records to machine-readable form, thereby recataloging the entire collection. This corrects or eliminates many of the historical idiosyncrasies of variant cataloging practice that have been created over the history of the library. This includes the adoption and implementation of all professional and technical standards of bibliographic control. Authority control systems for names, subjects, and the syndetic reference structure further refine this achievement.

2. A commonly cited objective is the integration of all bibliographic records for the library in a single enumerative, interactive catalog including such diverse

materials as audiovisuals, books, serials, maps, rare books, periodicals, documents, manuscripts, and all varieties of micromedia.

3. Automated systems provide integration of diverse collections in branches and departments throughout a multilibrary system in a single online public access catalog (OPAC). It is common that a main library catalog list the holdings of branch or departmental libraries. Rarely, though, does one find a branch library able to provide and maintain a complete catalog of the main library or other branches. Automated systems not only provide this capability, but concurrent circulation data on all materials can be observed on any system terminal.

4. The reduction of repetitive or redundant manual tasks in staff work is achieved. The preparation of multiple card sets is, thankfully, one of the first casualties of even the most fundamental of automation activities, namely, shared cataloging databases. This common change is frequently cited as an example of how cataloging processing time can be reduced, improving technical services through speed. In a more complex example, automation with integrated systems can coordinate the activity of acquisitions and cataloging functions by creating the basic bibliographic record for cataloging purposes as a book order is searched in the system prior to the ordering of the work from the publisher. Simultaneously the purchase order is prepared, payment notation recorded, and appropriate reductions in book fund accounts made. Users of the system catalog also see the library as an active, demand-oriented organization, not merely a reactive archive that does not reveal its actions until they are complete.

The integration and coordination of acquisition and cataloging functions via a centralized database structure greatly improve the work flow. The organizational implication for planning and management is the need to reconcile and blend these previously distinct functions.

5. Greater staff productivity through the elimination of routine record management is commonly afforded by online library systems. Sorting, filing, and compiling circulation data and preparing overdue notices become an off-time, background process under automation, not someone's life work. Similarly, filing in or other maintenance of card format catalogs is eliminated by computer systems that do some of their best work while sorting.

6. As a system by-product, management information reports improve in precision and scope. This can lead to better decision making, planning, and scheduling. Control, if not the reduction, of unit and task costs becomes at least a realistic possibility with library automation. This area is one of the more commonly touted benefits of automation, but one of the least provable. The reality of this situation suggests that by eliminating some functions that are highly time consuming, such as those mentioned above, the library has the opportunity to shift staff to more productive, intellectually demanding tasks, as well as providing greater speed in the overall completion of work.

7. Accurate and contemporaneous record keeping becomes a reality with the installation of online systems. The practice of user and use analysis becomes a

more precise factor that can be used to influence, inform, and direct the conduct of library practice.

8. Automated systems provide greater precision in the user's perception of collection information. In dynamic, real-time systems users are immediately informed of ownership, location, and availability. This simple help is one of the most appreciated changes that patrons enjoy. Such added services as improved charging and discharging, recall notices, hold requests, and fine and payment control are subsumed under automatic processing routines.

9. Integrated systems provide multiple, simultaneous access and use of the system and its database independent of library location via remote access, dial-access, and quasinetwork relationships. Through simple electronics the system is as full and complete to personal users or libraries many miles distant as it is to staff in the next room. This level of full, concurrent disclosure is not possible without automation.

10. Access links from the local library to other local, regional, and national libraries via technological interaction and large-scale network resource sharing become functional parts of the library's design. Some sophisticated library systems allow not only local library searching but automatic switching to other automated systems in a network, triggering interlibrary loan transactions. This level of system interaction promotes the last of our objectives.

11. The demand model of information access is created in contrast to the historic, archival model. With the assist of automated systems, library resources are truly no longer bound by the confines of local ownership.

In the foregoing list, which is by no means intended to be exhaustive, one can recognize at least one salient issue: change. Two points are of critical importance here. First, the goal of library automation is not the electronic rendering of manual activities themselves. Though it will inevitably occur, it is not the goal. What is the goal is the improvement of library service and operation. This can be accomplished by the improvement of throughput in processing queues, better record keeping, the freeing of valuable staff time for higher-order service and technical activities, and better management control over library systems and services. Cost reduction, as such, does not appear on the list, for in reality it probably will not occur in a direct causal relationship.

Second, change in and of itself is a powerful force in the lives of all. Its influence must be managed like automation itself. Communication with all levels of staff, consultation with those to be affected by the process, and integration of their ideas in the design, specification, and evaluation of the project are essential. Managing the automation project to accomplish changing practices will require putting concepts into practice, putting information science in library service, and putting systems into the library methodologies of evaluation, analysis, and design.

Library Automation Comprehensive Planning

Comprehensive planning is the foundation of library automation. Library automation comprehensive planning is the activity of identifying, specifying, and selecting the goals, objectives, and alternative courses of action for accomplishing the mission of the library. As such it is similar to other long-range planning activities, and its significance is as fundamental as any strategic planning activity. Under good management it should help anticipate the effect of decisions, indicate the financial consequences of various alternatives to action, and in general focus on the broad spectrum of programs, procedures, practices, and interrelationships in the library.

The planning processes should also indicate the methods of support (both internal and external), whether these be human, material, or financial, available to the library and should then link them with the costs to be incurred. The costs themselves should be a major component of the planning activities, and the importance of elaborating these should be a central consideration. The traditional strategic planning model is entirely appropriate for the library approaching a major automation project. As such it will serve as a template for the process.

The planning process itself must be planned, and the development of this process must begin with identification of the goals, objectives, and tasks toward which the process is directed. The goals and objectives must be supported by a rationale for automation in general, plans for its development, and the methods for its implementation. The planning process should identify the tasks to be performed and those on whom this responsibility rests. Ultimately the library administrator is responsible for creating and supporting the environment of planning. This role may be delegated to a single planning officer or system specialist, or the library may choose to solicit the participation of an outside consultant to provide additional human resources and expertise either as an initiating force or on a continuing basis.

In all reality, whether recognized as such or not, the library has already begun the planning process by the act of stating its organizational mission, goals, and objectives. Even if no formal statement of this philosophical structure exists, it does exist in a *de facto* manner through the structure, function, and activities of the library. Planning must begin with this statement essentially describing where the library is headed. The library's planning process for automation will refocus attention on these relevant ideas and begin reinterpreting the goals and objectives in view of automation.

In library automation planning the need for the linkage of mission, goals, and objectives is perhaps more essential than in some other undertakings. The planning process, its understanding, and coordination can serve to integrate and make coherent the variety of activities in disparate departments within the organization and focus attention on the larger task. As libraries move toward integrated systems, with computerization serving as the unifying vehicle, the work flow and the end product become directly linked and interrelated in a way that was probably not hitherto possible. More than ever before the actions, procedures, and decisions made by one department can and will come to influence the work of other departments in a manner that can be more readily perceived.

Library automation activities transcend several, if not many, annual budget cycles. Therefore, the planning process should be structured to realistically address this time duration. Specifically, planning on the basis of near-term objectives and budgeting for them accordingly not only can mark incremental successes but can also effectively bring to bear library resources, staff, and money toward task completion.

Successful planning for library automation activities should observe these characteristic principles:

1. The planning activity must reflect a total commitment of the library administration and staff to the overall success of the project. Library system development cannot be ultimately successful if one or more departments are nonparticipants or are openly opposed to automation.

2. This planning process and the activity at which it is directed must be supported by the external governance structure to which the library is responsible and accountable. The role of the library leadership is crucial, requiring timely, authoritative, and realistic presentations to the governance authorities.

3. The planning process must be directed at generating action toward completion of the project. It must not be viewed as an idle, theory-based, wishful-thinking exercise.

4. The planning process itself should be carefully organized and capable of continuity over an extended period of time (five years or more) addressing changes to be made, milestones to be marked, and decision and action levels to be achieved. Its progress should be reviewed periodically (at least annually), modified as necessary, and communicated to all affected parties both internally and externally.

5. Responsibility for the activity and direction of the planning activity should be vested in a single coordinator capable of effectively managing, integrating, and representing the discrete and unique planning components from various departments and interest groups. It is incumbent upon this individual to facilitate the process, provide cohesive and coherent direction toward project success, and most important provide for continuity and progress over the life of the project.

6. It must be understood that the key factor in library automation planning is the functional involvement of all levels of staff and all departments of the library. Planning for automation should be comprehensive in scope, strategic in nature, and focused on overall integration of all activities and departments in the context of the total library operation.

7. Planning should be integrated with library administration and management. This principle is especially true regarding budgeting, system finance, specification and evaluation of bids, contract satisfaction, and system performance. The planning process, the library administration, and automation management must be coordinated and structured to provide for adequate checks and balances that lead to responsible execution of plans and realistic expectations.

8. Planning activities should be supported by an adequate information base that includes explications of various alternatives and a means for cooperative evaluation of each contingency. This planning information base should include analyses of existing systems, projected trends under current conditions, as well as projections of changes expected from the automation implementation.

9. Resources for planning must be provided and adequately maintained. Good planning, as expensive as it is, is far less expensive than the results of making decisions and purchases in the absence of planning. Costly errors and embarrassing outcomes can be avoided when judgments are based on complete studies, thorough analyses, and fully reasoned, unhurried conclusions.

10. Planning by individual units must parallel system planning and lead to integration with all other departmental and functional activities in the library. Isolation of unit-based planning must be avoided, and it is the responsibility of the planning officer to solicit, identify, and accommodate various planning perspectives.

A good planning process cannot in itself guarantee a successful project; but poor planning will assure disappointment and failure.

Functional Components of Library Automation

It is entirely too easy to be consumed by the bits and pieces of automation systems. Automation systems are frequently described as an accumulation of hardware, software, and databases. While all of that is true, it is also false on the side of simplicity. What are the components of library automation? The list is lengthy, but it can be grouped in aggregates of related attributes. First, there is the hardware with the necessary characteristics of reliability, flexibility, and expandability and a history of performance that will inspire confidence. Second, we must include software based on a competent operating system arranged around sound principles of database management that is also an efficient user of system resources in a multitasking, multiuser environment. The database is actually a group of databases that must interact flawlessly and cogently, linking users to materials, libraries to users, and the library to other libraries and external services via the software and hardware, all in a real-time, dynamic system.

These are the elements of automation that a library will install when the decision is made to "go online." These are the superficialities of automation, the bells and whistles that are tangible, usable, and high profile. These are the externally provided, paid for, and delivered products of automation.

Beneath the surface, though, reside the depth and reality of library automation. First and foremost are the human components, the library staff replete with its technical skills, cooperative needs and opportunities, professional knowledge, and analytical insight. No matter how good the system is when the plug goes in the socket, if the staff cannot, or is unwilling to, make it do the job, the system is worthless.

Second, there is the material that is owned by the library. It will be represented in the bibliographic database, but it is important to bear in mind that the system is there to represent library materials, not bibliographic records. Books, audiovisuals, periodicals, documents, maps, manuscripts, and all other materials require full and accurate representation. The size, type, and use of the collection will determine the nature of the automation system.

Third, automation represents significant financial realities for the library, exceeding in scale all other activities in most libraries with the exception of the building itself. In addition to the purchase price for the system, there will be additional costs for site preparation, database development, and eventually ongoing costs of maintenance, use, and system enhancement.

Fourth, there is the need for staff training and development to enhance and modify skill levels for transition to the automated system. In some instances this step will necessitate the adoption of new or variant routines while other more complex activities may arise that require a structured and analytical process of redesigning tasks and procedures. This aspect has bearing on both those individuals involved and the library administration and management. The organizational structure must accommodate not only the need for these changes, but the relative impact on those whose daily work lives are affected.

Fifth, no significant library automation system can be installed without changes in the physical plant itself. Space must be provided for the computer equipment, plans must be made for the environmental protection of that equipment, and the specifics of system layout and configuration must be provided. The library may be limited in its location of the equipment, but the needs of the users and staff for the equipment must be a central consideration. The library may decide to undertake use studies to identify traffic patterns in various locations of the library to determine the best locations for peripheral devices. Site preparation must also be arranged in such manner as to keep at a minimum the disruption to ongoing services and activities.

Sixth, the record keeping activities of the library, and the records themselves, will influence the automation process. The library should assess those records that have been gathered and maintained in the paper-based system, in view of those functions of the online system that will either not need those records or will keep those records as part of the system itself. In some instances this will free the staff from certain activities traditionally performed.

Seventh, the procedural flow of activities and materials in the library will be subject to review, analysis, and modification. The important characteristics of such inquiry are two-fold. These procedures have developed over a long period of time and as such have a long history based in the work flow of the organization. Also, these procedures are the end-product of the staff members' own interpretation of their jobs and tasks. Both of these attributes tend to dictate a historical pattern or traditional behavior that is indigenous to the library. These attitudes and traditions can stand as a significant barrier to the adoption of new systems, if there is not careful attention to staff-centered needs, both professional and personal.

Eighth, an important automation function that must be integrated into the system design is the technological options that are available to, and required by, the library. As the automation project advances an appropriate linkage and integration must be formed among these less tangible components of library systems, the availability of funding, the application of desired elements, and the planning, review, and evaluation activities needed for all of these elements to coalesce into a single library system.

When considering the options for the system design it is important that the library review not only what is needed by the library, but what is desired for the service to the clientele. This in mind, the library will find it advisable to study the use patterns of the library and branches where applicable to determine what the users find desirable.

The need to set options and make choices pervades modern systems approaches to automation in general and, in this case, in libraries in particular. Merely providing ample descriptive options for variant library media formats illustrates this point. Descriptions of categories of library users, loan periods, points of bibliographic access, branch locations, and the existence of multiple copies are included on any list of specific needs each library should be able to define individually. The notion of one system for all libraries is anathema. Libraries, for all their similarities, are incredibly diverse in their practices. Automation systems must accommodate these variations. So important is this consideration that the variety of system options should become a primary evaluation point.

Additionally, system performance, system capacity, and system size will function to limit the ultimate size of the database without changes in capacity, equipment, or even vendors and product lines. The elaboration of the database will impact the throughput speed of the processing unit while developing the database. Therefore choices must be made and priorities set as the database is designed.

For example, the MARC record has come to stand as the archetype of the complete and thorough bibliographic record. Its use and value for catalogers and acquisition personnel are commonly accepted. On the other hand, its complexity is wholly inappropriate for a user who simply wants to read a book. Clearly the solution is to provide both; most online systems can accommodate this articulation of the database for variant user and staff needs.

Procedural Overview

The actual task of automating the library system will follow a general pattern of planning and activity. The assumption at this point is that the decision to automate has been made and the initial approval for this activity has been secured. The relative speed with which the process will go forward will be influenced by the level and extent of financial and human resources available in any given time period. The overall pattern of the work to be done is largely the same for all libraries:

1. The library must identify the staff members and other specialists who will be responsible for the process itself. This may involve the formation of a committee drawn from various departments in the library, and it may include the designation of a systems specialist or coordinator to guide the process. Selection and contracting of consulting services should happen at this time, if it is deemed necessary to the overall project. In any event the leadership of the project must be identified and given the authority to draw together talent and resources equal to the task.

2. The second task is the identification, preparation, and coordination of the bibliographic database which will form the central, functioning component of any library automation system. The precise definition, content, and use mechanisms of this database must be determined by the local staff. In its simplest form, any bibliographic database will include the standard bibliographic identifiers.

The preparation of the database can be the single most time-consuming task in automation. In cases of libraries that have not already created a machine-readable database via a cataloging system such as OCLC, this project must be started immediately. External, third-party vendors can be contracted or other products or services acquired which will facilitate this activity.

3. The next task to undertake in this automation process is the analysis of the library itself. In this regard the planners should evaluate, measure, and describe the library collection, the users, and the uses that are made of the resources. Staff function, processes, and procedures should be diagrammed, explained, and evaluated for their content, importance, and connection to other processes and departments. This step should conclude with a series of statements indicating those procedures that should be retained, those that can be deleted, and those that can be retained only with modification as the library begins to automate.

4. A fourth task is the investigation and observation of existing automated systems in libraries of similar size and use. Part of this process is the initial contact with potential automation vendors to gather information on the general characteristics, services, and components of their systems. The relative cost of the variously configured systems will begin to frame in the general cost factors that will be encountered in the actual bidding process. The library literature will identify automation activities and suppliers whose information should be gathered and analyzed for application to the current project.

5. The process of querying vendors for information can be handled very informally; so, too, may be the vendor's response. Using a request-for-information (RFI) procedure will formalize this process without commitment and greatly increase the quality and validity of the responses. An RFI is generally brief, a few pages at most, stating the general need, intent, and characteristics of the library including type, size, growth rate, clientele, and desired functions. A typical vendor response would indicate interest, applicability, options, and cost guidelines. Some vendors could respond with detailed statements of capability and helpful hints or guidelines for the automation novice.

Just as no two libraries are the same, no two installed automation systems are the same. What should be studied are patterns of problem resolution and satisfaction. The ability to vary, adapt, and expand systems to match local needs is a direct object of inquiry and evaluation. The breadth of application of installations and their success speaks powerfully for the experience level, versatility, and design competence of the vendor and this system in general. It is important to bear in mind that the task at hand is information gathering.

6. The next step in this process is the bringing together of the library automations planning staff from all departments. Their collective task is to formulate in real terms, in formal presentations, with full justification and explanation, all of

the various components of the developing design for the automation system that they seek, need, demand, and expect. They are stipulating what they expect to find represented in any selected automation system.

For example, the catalogers must specify and design the components they perceive for the improvement of their work environment not only to their own satisfaction, but to the satisfaction of others in the library as well. The circulation department must describe the nature and extent of record keeping, inventory control, and reporting function that must be retained, expanded, or modified under automation. The reference and other public service departments charged with responsibility for representing the library, the automation system, and the online database to the public must specify the necessary data elements, the display modes, and online helps the system should provide. Also important is the need for accuracy in the current holdings information which should be specific to the individual item or piece of material.

Critical in all system design and specification areas are the issues of human-system interaction. How is a book charged? How does the patron search by title, author, subject, or format, while limiting by year or language? How does anyone know if a particular work is currently available? How does everyone learn any of this? All of these and many more questions are relevant to both design and, eventually, evaluation. Only the local library, by understanding its resources, users, and uses, can decide the value of alternative solutions to this problem of human-machine interfaces.

7. The seventh step in this process should be the initial designation of the physical accommodations for the computer system itself. Computers, just like people, need their space, and the space needs of computer systems bear some special attention. The specific requirements of any system will vary in detail from one supplier to another, but the basics are quite similar. Computers need cool, clean, humidity-controlled, power-protected, secure spaces in which to operate.

8. The eighth step in this process is the library-based, staff-authored integration of the foregoing research and study activity into a single, comprehensive planning document that details the operating specifications for the automation system itself. These system specifications will constitute a thorough rewriting of the library operation and all of its functional elements. It will be a unique and custom design.

This final planning document should be detailed and comprehensive. It will be grounded in information storage and retrieval theory, database design and management concepts, and the measurement and evaluation of library systems and services. These technical and theoretical foundations are all directed at providing a system that acknowledges and asserts the value of human factors design principles to reinforce and substantiate the dominant service philosophy. Taken together, this document also demonstrates the application of library management theory both in its content and its process of development. At best it should be completely independent of any existing automation system or product line. At the same time it must be wholly integrated with the library itself.

Library automation systems, therefore, represent the grounding in reality of all of the theoretical foundations of library and information science. Automation does so perhaps more than any other single library activity. In library automation systems are found the tangible, functional, and usable attributes of theory. All library automation systems exist as variant approaches to the solution of the ultimate library issue: how is the user served best? The degree to which any system design resolves that issue is a matter for management and decision making.

Acquiring the System

Progress to this point does not prohibit the library from seeking the design and development of a custom library automation system. If the planning documentation is highly developed, this is precisely the time to exercise that option. Depending on the special circumstances of the individual library such a custom design may prove a viable alternative. The trend in the library profession, however, is to select from the many existing turn-key systems currently available, and, utilizing the flexibility of the local options-setting features of these products, create a locally specified system. Other than cost, the principal drawback of custom system development is the development time involved for programming, design specification, and debugging of what is essentially an experimental system design. To many, this activity now rivals reinventing the wheel.

Dealing with Automation Vendors

The formal specification of a proposed library automation system created by the library from its analytical and planning activities will form the majority of the content of the library's request to potential vendors or suppliers with systems to offer. The document will provide information to the vendors specifying the nature of the library and legal requirements for bidding. The request for proposal (RFP) created by the library will contain several specification components. It will contain requests for specific costs, maintenance availability, and training support. The RFP will also specify the nature and type of the system sought by the library. This request will also inform the vendor of the evaluation and performance tests that will be applied to any installed system. It is essential that this document be exhaustive, intentional, explicit, and precise in both concept and content.

In elaborating the procedural and information components of the RFP, the document should specify the explicit functions to be provided by the automated system. General system standards should be specified including the source and processing needs of the bibliographic database, its relevant access points, and performance standards including all interactions, integrations, and throughput capabilities. Processing time and protocols and the requirements for the maintenance of real-time, dynamic system records in all the variety needed by the library must also be stipulated. The system configuration with all its necessary components, peripherals, and interfaces should be explicitly detailed. The various databases required by the library and to be created by the online system should be detailed, and all necessary interrelationships should be elaborated.

The full range of circulation functions must be detailed. Most systems sought in this day and age will also include the functions of an online catalog. In this category of requirements, the system should provide access to the bibliographic database in the traditional approaches of author, title, and subject as well as format, language, publication year, publisher, or any other point of access desired by the library. The proposed system should be required to provide not only a variety of reporting mechanisms but also the details of how those records are maintained, processed, and reported. Any applicable statistical reporting information and its method of derivation are all important to this proposal.

Part of the language of the request for proposal should be a statement of defined terms. This is especially true in areas where there is legitimate opportunity for differences of opinion and different points of factual occurrence. Regardless of how the term is ultimately defined or agreed upon, everyone involved should at least be clear on the operant meaning. For example, response time is a critical evaluation point. The library may make statements asserting that system response time to a certain command should be within, say, two seconds. What is meant by response? The vendor may argue that the response by the computer itself is virtually instantaneous, a fact that is largely immeasurable and therefore indisputable. The library may intend that the response be visually confirmed on the screen of a visual display terminal, or that the result of the command be received at the terminal within that time. These three events are far apart in some instances, if not most. Careful definition of these key terms will eliminate or minimize unnecessary and avoidable arguments at a later time.

As stated above, the RFP should reveal and demonstrate the intentions of the design. These intentions must be realistic expectations based on computer technology. It is appropriate to push toward expansive and elaborate systems. It is inappropriate to expect that every dream will find a precise representation in an operating system.

The Bidding Process

Following the successful specification of the proposed system in the form of the request for proposal, the RFP is submitted to the appropriate automation system vendors for their responses. Typically, thirty days are allowed for the vendors to prepare their responses. Individual requirements of the bidding institution or library will vary with the institution, and there may be a formally stated purchasing procedure that must be followed. This procedure should be part of the bid request document itself provided to the vendors. A reasonable amount of time should be provided. This is especially true when one considers that the library may have spent months or years preparing the RFP itself. It is only fair to allow the vendor adequate time to respond.

When the bid responses are received, the first step in the evaluation of the bid is to examine the bottom line cost for the system. Only those bidders who fall within the library's budget for automation are considered to have provided a valid bid. The institutional budget for this project will be determined, in part, by the library staff based on its investigations, and partly on the basis of the funding that is available. This budget is not as much of a guessing game as it may appear. These system costs are estimable on the basis of research and previously submitted, nonbinding requests for information (RFI) mentioned earlier.

From the valid bid responses the library staff then enters into the phase of the process that is perhaps the most critical. Nonprofit, public, governmental, and educational institutions are commonly required to operate under the best and lowest bid formula for the acquisition of externally provided systems and services. The best and lowest bid formula is commonly and unfairly maligned in institutional purchasing practices. The actual goal of the best and lowest bid process is to provide the greatest opportunity for the organization to acquire the best available system, service, or product. The lowest bid is easy to comprehend—namely, the lowest price. The best bid side of the linkage is somewhat more complex but is designed by the library itself in the form of the system specifications.

The actual structure of the bid returned by the vendors may vary, but the content should be reflective of the individual specification provided by the library. There should be an exhaustive response to all components of the library system, indicating compliance with the requirements of the system and the degree to which that compliance is available, and clearly identifying any areas where variant options are either available, available with modification or additional cost, or not available at all either now or in the future.

The bid document should also contain a clear itemization of the incremental and collective costs for all system components, including optional components, software, features, documentation, training, maintenance contracts, and allied services to be provided by the vendor. Costs for insurance, delivery, and performance bonds should not be charged back to the library. Those are normal business costs for the suppliers and are not acceptable as bid components to individual purchasing libraries. The library should specify, and the bidders respond accordingly, that all bids are for complete, functional systems as bid and in compliance with the specifications. Some would argue that this should be implicit. That may be true, but automation is not an implicit business; it is painfully explicit and should be approached as such. Finally, all bid responses, costs, and services must be guaranteed for a definite time. Three months is customary, but this deadline may vary.

Evaluating the Bid

A careful, analytical, and intentional bid evaluation process, organized around a well-crafted bid document will uncover any discrepancies, shortcomings, or specific failures on the part of the vendor. The evaluative and analytical skills of the library staff are of paramount significance at this juncture. The concept of the best bid is to find the best combination of systems, services, and equipment that will fulfill the obligations and requirements that the library has specified. The library staff must systematically analyze the content of the bid document for points of satisfaction of the specifications.

Simply put, if the library specified that the proposed system is to have the capacity for a certain number of bibliographic records, then there should be found explicit responses by the bidder that the system will in fact contain those records. Furthermore, the relationships of various databases, processes, and activities within the system and supported by the procedural environment in the library itself must also be carefully delineated by the bidder. Not all system specifications are of equal importance, and the library staff members should carefully, if only among themselves, identify those elements of the proposed system that can be accepted with modification, or entirely omitted, if the need arises. Intent and performance criteria must be represented adequately and to satisfaction. Part of this process is the reservation on the part of the library to solicit explanations for any questioned areas, to demand real-time demonstrations provided by the vendor, and, ultimately, to reject any and all bids if the library's specifications or concept is not fulfilled.

The bid should be evaluated thoroughly on each element specified. Frequently, a bid evaluation document is prepared following each point in the RFP. This evaluation document demands that each specification be directly addressed; individual response items may be classed as essential, preferred, or optional. The degree to which each aspect is provided by the vendor's system can be indicated as either available, available as an added option, not yet available but planned (with specific date), or not available and not planned. Using a weighted scoring system will objectively score each section of the bid and provide a combined score for the total system. These bid scores will provide a ranking for the various bids.

This quantitative process, if properly administered, weighted, and scored, will provide a sound basis for system comparisons. It is not the intent of this process to render all of the creative system design work in a numerical matrix. The evaluation document and process can easily provide for qualitative assessment. Representative comments could be stated as "screen instructions are easily understood by first-time users" or "command and menu language is mnemonic" or "search results are displayed with easily identified field labels." The bid analysis process is intended to fairly evaluate each competing system on its performance measures as defined by the library as evaluation criteria, be they qualitative or quantitative. It is also intentionally designed to eliminate or minimize any biases or prejudices that exist.

The bidder must clearly show, and make affirmative statements concerning, individual specifications to the end that there is no doubt about what is actually being bid. It should be borne in mind that the RFP and its bid response will form the basis of a contractual arrangement and legally binding document that will determine the nature of the system as installed, implemented, evaluated, and accepted. Contractual negotiations may clarify, eliminate, or add certain aspects to the system specifications and costs. Those negotiations are within the scope of bid evaluation, but each point will have overall impact on the cost, perform-ance, and configuration of the system.

Library automation suppliers, like other computer sales representatives, are sometimes accorded the degree of trust and respect usually reserved for used car salesmen. This is probably an unwarranted oversimplification, but in reality, automation providers are in business. Libraries should not be surprised to find evidence of profit in this enterprise. The degree to which this profit is warranted in view of the delivered system is a matter for deliberation, but not the fact that it exists. Perhaps the best guideline for dealing with the sales representatives is to be firm but fair. The library has worked long and hard to determine the preferred configuration of the system that will answer its needs. If the vendor can provide all or part of the preferred arrangement, the library should negotiate in good faith to a satisfactory resolution of contractual disagreements. Vendors should behave similarly. Failure to do so obviates the need for further discussion on either part. Negotiation is useful toward an acceptable conclusion, but not as an activity in and of itself.

Part of the evaluation process is to investigate and evaluate the vendor. What is the historical pattern of business practices and customer satisfaction experi-enced by the vendor? Is the company a sound and profitable business? What assurances are there for continuing support, growth, and development? What are the company's research and development goals, plans, and activities? It is not only prudent but wise to elicit these answers by whatever means necessary.

Implementation and Evaluation

Upon successful completion of the bid evaluation process and its attendant contractual negotiations, the library and vendor together enter the implementa-tion phase. The involvement of the staff now becomes very directed at its own newfound tasks. Implementation must be closely tied to evaluation of the system as installed. All acquired knowledge must now be focused on this particular configuration.

System evaluation and final acceptance proceed together. If the preliminaries of planning were conducted properly, this task serves as verification. If this verification process is not successful, the library must vigorously pursue resolu-tion. It is important to remember that the actual evaluation of the system will not be complete until it is installed, the database is loaded, and the full system is functioning in the library. Only then can valid performance tests be conducted and the system evaluated against previously specified criteria. If these criteria are met, the system can be considered acceptable and the contractual requirements fulfilled. Appropriate performance tests should be designed in view of standards specified in the request for proposal or final contract. Final acceptance and payment for the system should not be made until these tests are passed.

Summary

As stated throughout this chapter, the significance of much automation activity resides in the library's pervasive, comprehensive transition, if not upheaval, from traditional, familiar, manual systems to nontraditional, unfamiliar, automated systems. What should be remembered are several salient points:

1. The mission, goals, and objectives of the library and its relation to its service community remain fundamentally unchanged.
2. The principles of librarianship, library service, and information science (including collection building, bibliographic access, research services, and physical access) are unchallenged.
3. Practices, procedures, work flows, staffing needs and patterns, and productivity will change dramatically.
4. The opportunities and challenges presented to any library staff operating under the adoption of automated systems will be intense, threatening, and, in some cases, debilitating.
5. The cornerstone of successful automation is effective management and leadership before, during, and after the arrival of the system.

The key to automation is planning. Planning is inherently administrative in nature. As an example consider the following scenario. Assuming no problems or delays in this process, which begins with the design and specification process, the RFP should be ready in no more than a year. Bidding, evaluation of the bids, site visits, deliberations, and negotiations will consume six months. Add another six months for site preparation, installation, and basic training. Loading the full database and linking records to materials should be done within another year. The full system can be loaded and operational one year after installation. By the time the system is ready for the first overdue notice, three years have passed since specification and two years since the bid. The fully operational system is, thus, three years older than the best plan and two years older than the best bid. Fully 40 to 60 percent of the system's five-year life span is past before the ribbon is cut. Is this a problem? Probably not. State-of-the-art and obsolescence are not as easily identifiable as one would expect. The point is that as the library goes online, the planning committee should be in session for the next system.

The value of long-term planning becomes even more apparent when the library is faced at some subsequent date with the need to upgrade, expand, or rebuild its system. Though good system selection in the beginning should have provided ample options for expansion and modification over time as the situation warrants, the reality of computer systems is that they will not serve forever. Eventually the system will have to be replaced with a newer, faster, bigger, and better system. No one seriously believes that the latest product announced will be the last one. Long-term planning activities will provide the opportunities for variant developments, anticipate needs before they are encountered, and smooth transitions from one system level to another.

Years after installation the planning process will address the problems of an exceeded limit on storage capacity, or a system load demand that outstrips the functional capacity of the processing unit. At a more basic level, problems with the system will arise, not in the form of a process that quits but more likely of a process that becomes necessary but cannot be provided. Ongoing planning and review processes will foresee these issues and, with the advantage of time, create the opportunity for flexible, innovative problem solving.

Further Reading

Corbin, John. *Managing the Library Automation Project.* Phoenix, Ariz.: Oryx, 1985.

DeGennaro, Richard. "Integrating Online Library Systems: Perspectives, Perceptions and Practicalities." *Library Journal* 110 (1 February 1985):37–40.

Drabenstott, Jon. "Funding Library Automation." *Library Hi Tech* Issue 13 (1985):111–119.

Fayen, Emily G. *The Online Catalog: Improving Public Access to Library Materials.* White Plains, N.Y.: Knowledge Industry, 1983.

Hildreth, Charles R. *Online Public Access Catalogs: The Use Interface.* Dublin, Ohio: OCLC, 1982.

Hoffman, Ellen. "Managing Automation: A Process, Not a Project." *Library Hi Tech* Issue 21 (1988):45–54.

Matthews, Joseph R. *Public Access to Online Catalogs: A Planning Guide for Managers.* Weston, Conn.: Online, Inc., 1982.

Reynolds, Dennis. *Library Automation: Issues and Applications.* New York: Bowker, 1985.

9

Measurement and Evaluation of Information Services

F. W. Lancaster

A typical dictionary may define evaluation as "assessing the value" of some activity or object. Authors dealing with the subject of evaluation, however, are likely to be more precise. Some claim that evaluation is a branch of research— the application of "the scientific method" to determine, for example, how well a program performs. Others stress its role in decision making: The evaluation gathers data needed to determine which of several alternative strategies appears most likely to achieve a desired result. Finally, some writers look upon evaluation as an essential component of management; in particular, the results of an evaluation may help the manager to allocate resources more effectively.

These various viewpoints, of course, are quite compatible. Moreover, they all tend to emphasize the "practical" nature of evaluation. An evaluation is performed not as an intellectual exercise but to gather data "useful" in problem-solving or decision-making activities.

A good way to focus on the evaluation of information services is through a generalized representation of the operations of an information center (or library) as seen through the eyes of an evaluator, as shown in Figure 9.1. The long-term objective of the center, presumably, is to produce certain outcomes in the community to be served. While certain desired outcomes will be the raison d'être for its existence, the center is more directly concerned with the processing of inputs in order to generate the outputs of the system, which are the information services it provides. The primary input, financial resources, is used to acquire major secondary inputs, namely information resources (mostly publications of various

This chapter, in substantially the same form, first appeared in the author's book *If You Want to Evaluate Your Library* (University of Illinois, Graduate School of Library and Information Science, 1988). It also incorporates material from two earlier papers: F. W. Lancaster and R. Mehrotra, "The Five Laws of Library Science as a Guide to the Evaluation of Library Services," in *Perspectives in Library and Information Science*, vol. 1 (Lucknow: Print House, 1983), 26–39; F. W. Lancaster, "Information as a Tool for Information Use," paper presented at the Nordic Seminar, Copenhagen, May 1985.

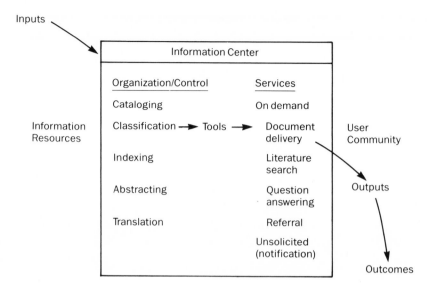

Figure 9.1. The operations of an information center

types), personnel to exploit these resources, and physical facilities to store materials, offer services, and so on.

The operation of the center can be considered as essentially a marriage between the information resources and the personnel: the system consists primarily of information resources and of people skilled in the exploitation of these resources on behalf of the users. Two principal groups of activities are identified in Figure 9.1 as taking place within the center. The first is concerned with organization and control of information resources. These activities—usually referred to as "technical services" in a traditional library setting—produce various tools (catalogs, bibliographies, shelf classification, and suchlike) that make possible the second group of activities, the public services.

The public services have been divided into two groups: "on-demand" services and "notification" services. The former can be considered passive services in the sense that they respond to demands rather than initiate them. The notification services, on the other hand, are more dynamic; they are designed to inform people of publications and other information sources likely to be of interest to them. The on-demand services themselves fall into two major groups: document delivery and information retrieval services. The notification services are primarily retrieval services or, more correctly, information dissemination services.

The center, then, can be considered as essentially an interface between the available information resources and the community of users to be served. Evaluation activities applied to the center should be concerned with determining to what extent it successfully fulfills this interface role.

Inputs, Outputs, and Outcomes

For evaluation purposes, an information center can be studied in a number of different ways. The diagram in Figure 9.1 implies that an evaluation program might look at inputs, at outputs, or at outcomes. The sequence "input, output, outcome" is one of increasing complexity. One would like to determine the extent to which the desired outcomes of a service have been attained. Unfortunately, the desired outcomes will tend to relate to long-term social, behavioral, or even economic objectives that are rather intangible and therefore not easily converted into concrete evaluation criteria. For example, a desired outcome in one institution might be "to improve the quality of teaching and research within the institution," while another might seek to "keep researchers and practitioners abreast of the latest developments in their fields of specialization."

Regrettably, while long-term objectives of this kind should provide the justification for the existence of information services, it is virtually impossible to measure the degree to which objectives of this type are reached. Even if the measurement were possible, one could not readily isolate the contribution made by the service itself. In short, one would do well to abandon the idea of using desired outcomes as direct criteria for the evaluation of information services. Drucker, in fact, has suggested that this situation will apply in the evaluation of any public service institution.[1]

In contrast to outcomes, the inputs of an information center are tangible and easily quantified. Indeed, both primary and secondary inputs are inherently quantitative rather than qualitative in nature. That is, the inputs have no value in and of themselves—they can be evaluated only in terms of the role that they play in achieving desired outputs.

The most obvious example of this, perhaps, is the collection of books and other materials that can be considered the major input to a library. Such collections cannot be evaluated in abstraction but only in relation to the purposes they are intended to serve and the actual needs existing in the population of potential users. In other words, the collection (input) must be evaluated in terms of the extent to which it satisfies the demands placed upon it (i.e., output); any other evaluation criteria would be artificial.

The outputs of the center—i.e., the services provided—are less tangible than the inputs but a lot more tangible than the outcomes. The outputs are easily quantified—e.g., number of documents delivered, number of referrals made, number of literature searches performed, number of questions answered—but this is not enough. Unlike inputs, the outputs of an information center can and must be evaluated in terms of quality. Thus, for each service provided, qualitative criteria of success should be identified.

This brings us back to the outcomes of an information service. While these cannot be studied directly, the criteria used to evaluate outputs should be good predictors of the extent to which the desired outcomes are achieved.

1. P. F. Drucker, "Managing the Public Service Institution," *The Public Interest* 33:43–60 (1973).

Take, for example, a current awareness service, such as a selective dissemination of information (SDI) system. The desired outcome is to make users better informed and more up to date in their areas of specialization. The achievement of this objective is not easily measured directly. However, the desired outcome strongly suggests what the evaluation criteria should be at the output level. It seems reasonable to assume that the more items the service brings to the attention of users that are directly related to their interests (and, conversely, the fewer that are not directly related), the more likely it is that the users become better informed. Further, the more of these items that are new to the user (i.e., items of which he or she was previously unaware), the more likely it is that the service is succeeding in keeping the user up to date. Thus, two evaluation criteria for this output (service)—relevance (or pertinence) and novelty—have been identified that seem also to be good predictors of the extent to which the desired outcome is reached.

Clearly, the interrelationship that exists among inputs, outputs, and outcomes has important implications for the design of information systems and services. One should begin by defining what it is that the system is intended to achieve. These are the desired outcomes. One then determines what services (outputs) are needed to produce these outcomes, and how these services can be provided most efficiently and economically. This leads to the identification of the inputs necessary to achieve the desired outputs. The criteria used to evaluate these services should predict extent of attainment of the outcomes that guided their establishment. For document delivery services, presumably, the output measure would be the number of document needs satisfied (i.e., the extent to which the service can supply publications to users at the time they are needed); for question answering services, it would be the percentage of questions answered completely and correctly; for referral services, it would be the percentage of referrals that lead users to appropriate sources of information. Literature searches would be evaluated in terms of the relevance of the results to the information needs of the users and, for certain types of needs, the completeness of the results. It should be noted that some information services can be evaluated on a binary scale—either the user does or does not get what was wanted. Others can be evaluated only according to some form of graduated scale—for example, the proportion of items retrieved in a literature search that is directly relevant to the needs of the requester.

Just as qualitative measures of output can predict achievement of outcomes, there exist certain input measures that might be considered good predictors of desired outputs. For example, the more items that exist within the collection of the center, the more document delivery needs are likely to be satisfied; the larger the collection of reference tools, the more questions that are likely to be answered completely and correctly; and so on.

Indeed, it is possible to use certain evaluation methods, applied to input, that are intended to simulate an output situation and thus to approximate an evaluation of output. For example, in evaluating the coverage of some portion of a collection against an external standard, such as an authoritative bibliography, one is in effect estimating the ability of the library to satisfy information needs of actual users in the subject. This approach is legitimate if one can be sure that the external standard fully reflects the needs of the users of this particular collection.

Costs, Effectiveness, and Benefits

A somewhat different way of looking at evaluation is in terms of costs, effectiveness, and benefits. Effectiveness relates to outputs, and the overall criterion of effectiveness is the proportion of user demands that is satisfied. The benefits of the system are really the desired outcomes. Costs are quite tangible as long as one thinks only in monetary terms. But it is easy to be myopic in this respect. One should avoid the fallacy that time spent using information services is free. User time is not free, at least not within the broad context of society as a whole. In point of fact, the cost of operating an information service may be quite small compared with the cost of using it. For certain evaluation purposes, a realistic cost analysis of an information service should take all costs—including those incurred by users—into account. This point will be pursued further later in the chapter.

At a national level, costs incurred by all components of the system may need to be considered. Suppose, for example, that an information center, A, requests photocopies of a particular periodical from other centers ten times a year. From A's point of view, it may be cheaper to do this than to subscribe to that periodical. However, from the viewpoint of the national system as a whole—taking the costs of all components into account—it may be cheaper for A to pay the subscription and handling costs.

Cost can be related to effectiveness or to benefits. Cost effectiveness refers to the costs of achieving a particular level of effectiveness within an information service. Some type of unit cost measure will be needed. Examples of cost effectiveness measures would include cost per document delivered to users, cost per question answered successfully, cost per relevant item retrieved in a literature search, and so on. The cost effectiveness of a service can be improved by holding costs constant while raising the level of effectiveness or by maintaining a particular level of effectiveness while reducing the costs.

Cost effectiveness, then, relates to optimization in the allocation of resources—the better the allocation of resources, the better the quality of service (i.e., effectiveness) that is achieved for a particular level of expenditure. In this connection, one must recognize that it is unrealistic to expect an information system to satisfy every need of every user. The concept of the 90 percent library is an important one.[2] That is, one can design a service that will satisfy some reasonable percentage of all demands—perhaps as much as 90 percent—but to go beyond that would require a completely disproportionate level of expenditure. For example, 200 periodical titles may satisfy 90 percent of the needs for periodi-

2. C. P. Bourne, "Some User Requirements Stated Quantitatively in Terms of the 90% Library," in A. Kent and others, eds., *Electronic Information Handling* (Washington, D.C.: Spartan Books, 1969), 93–110.

cal articles in a particular institution, but 500 may be needed to satisfy 95 percent of the needs, and 1,200 to satisfy 99 percent.

A cost-benefit evaluation relates the benefits (outcomes) of a service to the cost of providing it. Again, the cost-benefit relationship can be improved by increasing benefits without increasing costs or by reducing costs without reducing benefits. In the long term, however, a cost-benefit study attempts to demonstrate that the benefits derived from a service outweigh the costs of providing it. Because, as suggested earlier, the benefits of information services tend to be intangible, and not easily expressed in the same unit as the costs (e.g., dollars), true cost-benefit studies are virtually unattainable in our field. Nevertheless, attempts have been made, with varying degrees of success. Approaches used include those that try to justify the cost of an information service by:

1. Showing that, if an in-house information service did not exist, it would cost the organization more to buy the same level of service from outside sources.[3]

2. Proving that costly research may be duplicated if adequate information services are not available or are not used effectively.[4]

3. Showing that information services can improve the quality of decision making or can reduce the professional level of the staff needed to make various types of decisions.[5]

4. Showing that if an in-house information service were not available, costs to the organization would increase as engineers, scientists, or other professionals are forced to spend more of their own time in information-seeking activities with resulting loss in their own productivity.[6]

5. Proving that an information service has contributed tangibly to the organization (e.g., by helping to win a contract, by revealing cheaper solutions to research or production problems, or by stimulating the development of new products).

While most managers would like to be able to prove that the services they provide can be justified from a cost-benefit point of view, the difficulties involved in such a study have discouraged all but a few attempts of this kind. For this reason, this chapter will focus on outputs and effectiveness rather than on outcomes or benefits.

3. D. Mason, "PPBS: Application to an Industrial Information and Library Service," *Journal of Librarianship* 4:91–105 (1972); M. S. Magson, "Techniques for the Measurement of Cost-Benefit in Information Centres," *Aslib Proceedings* 25:164–185 (1973).

4. J. Martyn, "Unintentional Duplication of Research," *New Scientist* 21:338 (1964).

5. A. M. McDonough, *Information Economics and Management Systems* (New York: McGraw-Hill, 1963).

6. K. C. Rosenberg, "Evaluation of an Industrial Library: A Simple-Minded Technique," *Special Libraries* 60:635–638 (1969); J. Kramer, "How to Survive in Industry: Cost Justifying Library Services," *Special Libraries* 62:487–489 (1971); M. W. Mueller, "Time, Cost and Value Factors in Information Retrieval," paper presented at the IBM Information Systems Conference, Poughkeepsie, N.Y., September 21–23, 1959.

Purpose of Evaluation

There exist a number of possible reasons why the managers of an information center may wish to conduct an evaluation of the services provided. One is simply to establish a type of "benchmark" to show at what level of performance the service is now operating. If changes are subsequently made to the services, the effects can then be measured against the benchmark previously established. A second, and probably less common, reason is to compare the performance of several information centers or services. Since a valid comparison of this type implies the use of an identical evaluation standard, the number of possible applications of this kind of study tends to be quite limited. Examples include comparison of the coverage of different databases, the comparative evaluation of the document delivery capabilities of several libraries, and the use of a standard set of questions to compare the performance of question-answering services. A third reason for evaluation of an information service is simply to justify its existence. A justification study is really an analysis of the benefits of the service or an analysis of the relationship between its benefits and its cost. The fourth reason for evaluation is to identify possible sources of failure or inefficiency in the service, with a view to raising the level of performance at some future date. Using an analogy with the field of medicine, this type of evaluation can be regarded as diagnostic and therapeutic. In some ways it is the most important type. Evaluation of an information service is a sterile exercise unless conducted with the specific objective of identifying means of improving its performance.

Evaluation Methods

Because each service presents a different set of problems, and a number of alternative evaluation procedures may exist for each, a review of evaluation methods relevant to all types of information services is well beyond the scope of a review of this type. Nevertheless, some very general principles are worth mentioning.

An evaluation of an information service may be subjective or objective. Subjective studies—based on opinions—are not without value because it is important to know how people feel about a service. But an evaluation is of most value if it is analytical and diagnostic, seeking to discover how the service might be improved, and it is difficult to base this type of study on opinion alone. In general, then, objective criteria and procedures should be followed. The results of an objective study should be quantifiable.

An objective evaluation is really concerned with establishing probabilities—for example, what is the probability that a library will own an item needed by a user, or what is the probability that a user's question will be answered correctly? These probabilities must be broken into component probabilities for evaluation purposes. Consider the following evaluation question: "What is the probability that a user seeking a particular book in a particular library will be able to walk out of the library that day with the book in hand?" The component probabilities are as follows. What is the probability that:

1. The library will own the book?
2. The user can find an entry for it in the catalog?
3. The book is on the shelf?
4. The user can find it on the shelf?

When this document delivery situation is dissected, a number of separate but interrelated evaluation situations become evident: collection evaluation, catalog use evaluation, and shelf availability studies. Each information service needs to be analyzed in a similar way if one is to fully understand the evaluation problems it presents.

Evaluation studies can involve real users in real institutional settings. Alternatively, various simulations are possible. If "real" studies are employed, the evaluator can try to get all users to participate on a voluntary basis or can use random sampling to focus on a set of representative users. The latter is much to be preferred. It is better to get reliable data from a few users than to gather less reliable data from many.

For certain evaluation purposes, too, it may be sufficient that evaluation data be anonymous while, for other purposes, this may not be good enough. For example, materials left on tables in a library may reflect materials consulted in that library but tell us nothing about who used them and for what purpose. Random interviews with people using materials within a library give qualitatively different data that may be essential in answering certain types of questions concerning in-house use of the collection.

If carefully designed, simulation studies can provide much valuable information without disturbing the users of the system at all. A good example is the "document delivery test."[7] A list of bibliographic references, say 300, forms the basis of a search in a particular library on a particular day. The search determines how many items are owned and how many of the items owned are actually available on the shelves. In effect, the test simulates 300 users walking into the library that day, each one looking for a single item. As long as the 300 references are fully representative of the needs of the users of that library (not too difficult to achieve in the case of a special library, much more difficult for a general library), the simulation can give excellent data on the probability of ownership and the probability of availability. Other simulations can be devised for other information services, including question answering and literature searching.

7. R. H. Orr and others, "Development of Methodologic Tools for Planning and Managing Library Services," *Bulletin of the Medical Library Association* 56:235–267 (1968).

The Five Laws of Library Science

Ranganathan's five laws of library science can guide decisions on what should be evaluated, by what criteria, and by what methods.[8] These laws provide a fundamental statement of the goals that information services should strive for, and they are as relevant today as they were fifty years ago.

The first law, books are for use, seems obvious, but it is a law that libraries don't always adhere to. Ranganathan himself deplored the fact that many librarians seemed to be more concerned with preservation than with use, thus perpetuating the image of the librarian as a custodian rather than as someone skilled in the exploitation of bibliographic resources. The most obvious implication of the law is that one must evaluate collections and services in terms of the needs of users. Moreover, it suggests that objective, empirical investigation should replace purely subjective or impressionistic approaches.

One objective approach to the evaluation of collections involves some form of "list checking"; that is, various bibliographies are chosen as standards by which to judge the strength of the collection in different subject areas. For certain evaluation purposes, some preexisting "standard" list might be suitable. In other cases, however, no useful standard list will exist. Nevertheless, it will frequently be possible to construct a special list to achieve the objectives of a particular study. The technique (as applied by Coale to the evaluation of library collections and by Martyn, and Martyn and Slater to the evaluation of the coverage of databases[9]) assumes that publications cited in recently published literature are among those that library users will be likely to ask for. To evaluate the holdings of a scholarly library in some subject area, a useful evaluation tool could be compiled from sources cited in the most recently published books and journal articles (especially review articles) in this subject area. In essence, by checking such a list against the holdings of a particular library, one is asking the question, "To what extent could this library have supported the research of these writers?"

An approach more obviously related to the first law, however, is the evaluation of the collection in terms of the use now made of it. The assumption is that present use is a good predictor of future use, an entirely reasonable supposition because of the built-in inertia existing within large communities of users.

It is important to recognize that the relative use of portions of the collection is more important than their absolute use.[10] In other words, the evaluator should seek to distinguish between expected behavior (in a probabilistic sense) and

8. S. R. Ranganathan, *The Five Laws of Library Science* (Bombay: Asia Publishing House, 1931) is discussed in F. W. Lancaster and R. Mehrotra, "The Five Laws of Library Science as a Guide to the Evaluation of Library Services," in *Perspectives in Library and Information Science,* vol. 1 (Lucknow: Print House, 1983), 26–39.

9. R. P. Coale, "Evaluation of a Research Library Collection: Latin-American Colonial History at the Newberry," *Library Quarterly* 35:173–184 (1965); J. Martyn, "Tests on Abstract Journals: Coverage, Overlap, and Indexing," *Journal of Documentation* 23:45–70 (1967); J. Martyn and M. Slater, "Tests on Abstract Journals," *Journal of Documentation* 20:212–235 (1964).

10. A. K. Jain, *Report on a Statistical Study of Book Use* (Lafayette, Ind.: School of Industrial Engineering, Purdue University, 1967).

actual behavior. Probabilistically, if five times more chemistry material than physics material is owned, one expects chemistry material will be used five times more than physics material. If it is, the relative use of these portions of the collection is just as one expects it to be. There is something wrong, however, if physics and chemistry material are used at equal levels.

The acquisition policies of a library can be monitored on a continuous basis by comparing actual use with expected use, subject by subject throughout the collection. This can be done by collecting two kinds of data:

1. The relative proportions of the collection occupied by materials on various subjects (defined by their classification numbers).
2. The relative proportions of the total circulation accounted for by materials on various subjects (again, defined by classification numbers).

This allows one to identify "overused" and "underused" classes, that is, classes used more or less than expected.[11] If this type of monitoring is performed continuously, it will also be possible to identify classes in which relative use is increasing and those in which it is declining. Collection development policies can be modified accordingly. An alternative procedure, which gives essentially the same results, is to perform regular counts, for each major subdivision of the classification scheme, of how many books are on loan and how many are on the shelves.[12] The classes most in demand are those in which the proportion of items on loan most exceeds the proportion on the shelves. It is these classes that seem in greatest need of strengthening, for it is these classes in which most "shelf bias" seems likely to occur; that is, a user looking for materials on these subjects will find that the books left on the shelves will be those that no one else wants to borrow.

Of course, circulation data alone give an incomplete picture of collection use. One also wants to know what materials are consulted in the library. This is more difficult. One problem is simply the definition of what constitutes a "use." Frequently, an in-library use study is performed by recording details of materials left on tables in the library. Here the definition of use is "carried to a table." If one merely wants to know what kinds of things are used in the library (e.g., which journals, which subjects), this definition is perfectly acceptable. On the other hand, if one wants an absolute count of amount of in-library use, the method is likely to give a substantial underestimate.[13] A more laborious but more satisfactory method is to interview people within the library, on a random sampling basis, to determine who they are and what materials they are using.[14]

11. F. W. Lancaster, "Evaluating Collections by Their Use," *Collection Management* 4:15–43 (1982).

12. A. W. McClellan, "New Concepts of Service," *Library Association Record* 58:299–305 (1956).

13. C. Harris, "A Comparison of Issues and In-Library Use of Books," *Aslib Proceedings* 29:118–126 (1977).

14. R. J. Daiute and K. A. Gorman, *Library Operations Research* (Dobbs Ferry, N.Y.: Oceana Publications Inc., 1974).

The controversial study performed at the University of Pittsburgh clearly confirmed that most of the use comes from a very small part of the collection and, in fact, many items purchased by a large library may never be used at all.[15] Critics counter this by claiming that a book not yet used might be "discovered" at some future date. This argument flies in the face of probability. If a book is not used in its first year in the library the chance that it will be used in the second year declines. If it is not used in the second year, the chance that it will be used in the third declines further, and so on, with the probability of use declining more rapidly as each year goes by.

The results of the Pittsburgh study, indeed, suggest that the collection evaluation need be less concerned with how much various books are used than with which books are used and which are not. This simplifies the evaluation procedure and allows it to be performed continuously. For example, before a volume is reshelved a pressure sensitive dot may be fixed to its spine. Different colored dots can be used, depending on whether the volume has been consulted in the library (e.g., left on the table) or returned from circulation. During the first few weeks, a lot of time is spent in dotting used volumes. Gradually, however, most volumes used will already have been dotted, and the work will taper off to almost nothing. The advantage of this technique is that a trip around the shelves will quickly reveal the used and the unused items.[16] It will also show things borrowed but not used in the library, and vice versa, and indicate for how far back a particular periodical title is still in demand.

Carried to its logical conclusion, "books are for use" implies considerations of cost effectiveness. Because of limited resources, $30 spent on a book that is little if ever used is $30 less available for an item (possibly a duplicate copy) of something that might be in great demand. In the operation of information services, expected "cost per use" must be of paramount concern in deciding which items to add to a collection and which not. This situation is changing, however, as more and more bibliographic resources become accessible through electronic networks. The obvious implication of this, of course, is that "ownership" per se is becoming less important in the evaluation of the resources of an information service. The evaluation criterion is "accessibility": can the service make an item accessible to a requester, at the time he or she needs it, from whatever source, in whatever acceptable form?

Ranganathan's second law, every reader his book, is a logical extension of the first. Data on books borrowed or used in a library have an obvious limitation: they reflect only successes and tell us nothing about failures. That is, a book used represents, in some sense, a success. But volume of use is relatively meaningless unless one can convert it into a "satisfaction rate." To

15. A. Kent and others, *Use of Library Materials: The University of Pittsburgh Study* (New York: Dekker, 1979).

16. W. M. Shaw, Jr., "A Practical Journal Usage Technique," *College and Research Libraries* 39:479–484 (1978); W. M. Shaw, Jr., "A Journal Resource Sharing Strategy," *Library Research* 1:19–29 (1979).

do this one must determine the probability that a user, looking for a particular item or materials on a certain subject, will find this item or materials available at the time needed. In other words, for everything looked for, how much is found (success), and how much is not found (failure)? The second law goes beyond collection evaluation and into the assessment of "availability." It is not enough that an item sought by a user is owned by the library; it must also be available when needed.

One approach to an availability study is the "document delivery test" as used by Orr and others and by De Prospo and others.[17] The method is similar to the collection evaluation approach used by Coale: a bibliography of items assumed to represent the needs of users is compiled and applied to a library to determine (1) what proportion of the items is owned, and (2) what proportion of the items owned is available to users.[18] As mentioned earlier, such a test is essentially a simulation. The results of such an evaluation can be presented as a series of probabilities. If 200 of 300 items are found to be owned by the library, the probability that the library will own a particular item sought by a user has been estimated to be 2/3 or .66. If 100 of the 200 are immediately available when looked for, the probability of availability of an item owned is .5. The product of these probabilities (i.e., .66 × .5, or .33) is the probability that a book will be both owned and available. In other words, based on this sample, it would be possible to say that a user faces a probability of .66 that a needed item will be owned by the library; if owned, the probability that it will be immediately available is .5; the probability that any item will be both owned and available is .33.

"Every reader his book" can be considered a generic label that really means "Every reader his need." It can be extended to other types of needs of library users—e.g., what is the probability of having a factual question answered completely and correctly? This, too, can be handled by a similar simulation procedure in which the evaluator tests the library through a set of questions for which answers are already known.[19] In this case, the reference questions may be put to the library by volunteers posing as real users. The library is evaluated in terms of the number of questions answered completely and correctly.

The document delivery test provides both a collection evaluation and a "shelf availability" study but leaves out one other important factor affecting success in library use, namely the catalog search. That is, it assumes that, if something is owned and on the shelf, the user will be able to find its shelf location through the catalog, which is not necessarily true. In fact, in large libraries with large and complex catalogs, users may frequently overlook entries *actually present* in the

17. Orr and others, 235–267; E. R. De Prospo and others, *Performance Measures for Public Libraries* (Chicago: Public Library Association, 1973).

18. Coale, 173–184.

19. T. Crowley and T. Childers, *Information Service in Public Libraries: Two Studies* (Metuchen, N.J.: Scarecrow Press, 1971).

catalog.[20] To get a complete picture of "availability," then, one needs to know how successful is a library user in a search of the catalog. In the past, studies of catalog use have usually been performed through conducting interviews with a random sample of catalog users. To get complete information, interviews need to be conducted with users before and after they search the catalog. Some supplementary information may also be obtained by observation. The replacement of card catalogs by access through computer terminals may raise the success rate in searches of even very large collections; it may also lead to alternative evaluation procedures (e.g., certain data can be collected by unobtrusive monitoring).[21]

Simulations such as the document delivery test offer great attractions, not least of which is their inherent simplicity and the fact that users of the library are not inconvenienced by their implementation. Some would claim, however, that simulations are inferior to the "real thing." The real thing, in this case, is an evaluation of the success of actual users within the library. This can be achieved only through the cooperation of these users. One way is simply to ask them to fill out a special form or card if they encounter a failure while visiting the library.[22] Failure could be defined as "item not found in the catalog" or as "item found in catalog but not on shelf." Again, the method has a notable limitation: it tells us of failures but not of successes. It is very difficult to calculate a "failure rate" from such a procedure. More complete information can be obtained by interviewing a random sample of users as they enter the library and again as they leave. Success rate can then be determined.[23]

Whatever evaluation method is used, it is important for the evaluator to determine the precise cause of each failure identified, for example:

1. Item not owned (a collection failure)
2. Owned but not cataloged
3. In catalog but not found by user
4. Found in catalog but not available to user
   a. Being used by someone else
   b. Not available for some other reason (e.g., being bound)
5. On the shelf but not found by user on the shelf.

20. American Library Association, *Catalog Use Study,* V. Mostecky, ed. (Chicago: American Library Association, 1958); R. Tagliacozzo and M. Kochen, "Information Seeking Behavior of Catalog Users," *Information Storage and Retrieval* 6:363–381 (1970); R. Tagliacozzo and others, "Access and Recognition: From User's Data to Catalogue Entries," *Journal of Documentation* 26:230–249 (1970); Ben-Ami Lipetz, "Catalog Use in a Large Research Library," *Library Quarterly* 42:129–139 (1972).

21. J. Specht, "Patron Use of an Online Circulation System in Known-Item Searching," *Journal of the American Society for Information Science* 31:335–346 (1980).

22. J. A. Urquhart and J. L. Schofield, "Measuring Readers' Failure at the Shelf," *Journal of Documentation* 27:273–276 (1971); J. A. Urquhart and J. L. Schofield, "Measuring Readers' Failure at the Shelf in Three University Libraries," *Journal of Documentation* 28:233–241 (1972); P. B. Kantor, "Availability Analysis," *Journal of the American Society for Information Science* 27:311–319 (1976).

23. J. Martyn and F. W. Lancaster, *Investigative Methods in Library and Information Science: An Introduction* (Washington, D.C.: Information Resources Press, 1981).

The third law, every book its reader, complements the second. In relation to the second law, the library's role is relatively passive. Assuming that a user makes a demand on the library's services, the evaluator is concerned with whether or not the demand is satisfied. But libraries need to be more dynamic institutions. An important function should be that of making people aware of new publications of possible interest to them. Libraries should be concerned with "exposure" as well as with "accessibility."[24]

The significance of the third law is that books need to find their potential users as well as users the books they need. One could say that, for every item acquired by the library (and even, to carry this to its logical conclusion, for every item published) there are potential readers existing in the community. A library should therefore be evaluated in terms of its ability to inform people of the materials of potential use to them.

This is not such an easy evaluation exercise and, as a consequence, it is one rarely attempted. One obvious facet is simply the extent to which the library is able to achieve penetration in the community served—the extent to which its services are known, for example. More specifically, however, evaluation should be concerned with how successful the library is in informing users of newly acquired materials. If it produces a "new book list," how widely is it disseminated? Does it produce "targeted" bibliographies (e.g., new books on gardening) and, if so, do these reach the audiences who will most benefit (in this case, perhaps, gardening clubs)?

In the case of special libraries and information centers a more personalized level of current awareness should be possible, perhaps achieved through the use of computers to match the profile of a user's interests against characteristics of newly published literature (i.e., selective dissemination of information). In this case, the evaluation criteria would be:

1. How much of what is brought to a user's attention is actually relevant to his or her interests?
2. How much of what is relevant was previously unknown to the user?
3. What proportion of the items brought to the user's attention does the user ask to see?

The fourth law, save the time of the reader, virtually pervades all the others. Information services must be concerned not only with satisfying needs but with satisfying needs as efficiently as possible. It is now well known that the accessibility of information services is the major determinant of their use. Someone is likely to judge a service to be "inaccessible" if it requires too much effort to use.[25]

24. M. Hamburg and others, *Library Planning and Decision-Making Systems* (Cambridge, Mass.: MIT Press, 1974).

25. C. N. Mooers, "Mooers' Law, or Why Some Retrieval Systems Are Used and Others Are Not," *American Documentation* 11:ii (1960); T. J. Allen and P. G. Gerstberger, *Criteria for Selection of an Information Source* (Cambridge, Mass.: Sloan School of Management, Massachusetts Institute of Technology, 1966). Another version appears in *Journal of Applied Psychology* 52:272–279 (1968).

A defect of many evaluations of library and information services is that they look upon user time as "free." This erroneous assumption completely invalidates certain cost-effectiveness analyses that have been performed. The time of users cannot be considered free since the time they spend using library materials could be spent in other and, in some cases, more productive ways. In their analyses of the scientific and technical communication system in the United States, King and others showed that the cost of using (i.e., reading) publications greatly exceeds the cost of producing and distributing them.[26] By the same token, the cost of using the library greatly exceeds the cost of the collection, staff, and physical facilities. This can be seen most clearly in the case of a library within industry or within a government agency. If a scientist or engineer visits the library to use materials for, say, one hour, it may cost the library $5 in staff time (to assist the user) and other resources expended, but it actually may cost the organization $50, when the user's time (including all overheads) is figured into the calculations.

In the evaluation of library services the time of the user must be given sufficient weight. Moreover, in the cost-effectiveness analysis of information services, all costs, including all user costs, must be taken into account. To do otherwise could lead to a completely erroneous conclusion. This can be shown by a very simple example. Suppose that a chemist (paid $20 per hour) can perform a successful search in an online database in 30 minutes. Suppose, further, that a librarian (paid $10 per hour) could perform the search for the chemist in about the same amount of time. If the chemist's time is not taken into account, one could say that the librarian's search costs the organization $5 more than the chemist's search. This is clearly unacceptable since the organization is paying the chemist $10 for the time spent performing the search. If one takes the chemist's search time into account, one might come to the conclusion that it is cheaper for the librarian to do the search ($5 as opposed to $10 in personnel costs). Again, this may be an erroneous assumption. Before the librarian can perform the search for the chemist, what it is that the chemist is seeking must be made clear. Perhaps it takes the chemist 15 minutes to describe the needs to the librarian (i.e., $5 in chemist time). Obviously, $2.50 in librarian time is consumed concurrently. Thus, the personnel cost of the search performed by the librarian in 30 minutes would actually be $12.50, whereas the cost of the chemist performing the search was only $10.

This illustrates the fact that an information service cannot be evaluated in isolation but must be looked at within the context of the larger community of which it forms a part. This is particularly to be borne in mind in any cost-effectiveness or cost-benefit analyses.

The fifth and final law, the library is a growing organism, indicates that the library must be willing to adapt to new conditions. This would include adaptability to changing social conditions and adaptation to technological change. For the evaluator, this implies examining how long the library takes to adopt innovation,

26. D. W. King and others, *Statistical Indicators of Scientific and Technical Communication,* vol. 2 (Rockville, Md.: King Research, Inc., 1976).

including adoption of new publication forms and new forms of information distribution. Modern computer and telecommunications technologies are changing our very concept of "library." Indeed, as mentioned earlier, providing some form of online access to materials on demand seems gradually to be replacing access through "ownership," particularly in research libraries. That is, access rather than ownership should be the main criterion by which a library's "resources" should be evaluated.

Libraries should also be evaluated in terms of the extent to which they are able to capitalize on the capabilities that technology provides them with. For example, one important advantage of automated systems is that, if properly designed, they can provide many data to aid decision making and generally to improve the management process. Another facet is the ability of a library to exploit technology in order to provide services that it had not been able to offer earlier (e.g., a high level of literature-searching support made possible by online access to a wide range of databases).

There is another aspect to adaptation that must be considered, namely the ability of the library to adapt to changing needs among its clientele. In this connection there is a danger that must be recognized and guarded against. Library services cannot be evaluated solely in relation to the demands placed upon them by present users. Such evaluation accepts demands at face value and assumes that these demands are coextensive with user needs, which is not invariably true. Moreover, present users of a library may have needs for materials or information that, for one reason or another, are never converted into demands on the library's services. Finally, there are people who make no use of the library's services. If evaluation focuses only on the demands (i.e., expressed needs) of present users, and fails to understand the needs lying behind these demands, if it ignores the latent needs that are not levied as demands, as well as the potential needs of present nonusers, the danger exists of creating a self-reinforcing situation, one in which the library is constantly improving its ability to respond to the present type of demand and, by so doing, perhaps reducing its ability to attract new users or new uses of the resources available. Such a library is far from being a growing organism.

The Need for Evaluation

Line has expressed the opinion that academic libraries (at least) do not observe Ranganathan's Five Laws.[27] Indeed, he maintains that they tend to observe their own set of five laws, more or less diametrically opposed to Ranganathan's, namely:

1. Books are for collecting
2. Some readers their books
3. Some books their readers

27. M. B. Line, review of *Use of Library Materials: The University of Pittsburgh Study,* by A. Kent and others, in *College and Research Libraries* 40:557–558 (1979).

4. Waste the time of the reader
5. The library is a growing mausoleum.

This may seem rather facetious. Nevertheless, there seems to be some truth in Line's claims. For many years, libraries operated in an environment largely free from objective evaluation. If few serious complaints were received one tended to assume that the service was satisfactory. Such an assumption was frequently erroneous, but librarians, lacking objective performance measures and methods, became somewhat complacent about their services. When objective procedures were first applied to library and information services, some of the results shocked many people—e.g., the finding that a user may have less than a fifty percent chance that a sought item is immediately available in a library, or less than a 60 percent chance that his or her factual question will be answered completely and correctly.

The fact is that evaluation is an essential element in the successful management of any enterprise. Ranganathan's fifth law provides the major justification for evaluative activities. Healthy growth implies adaptation to changing conditions, and adaptation implies evaluation to determine what changes need to be made and how they may best be accomplished. Electronic technology has already produced new forms of publications and new media for the distribution of publications and information. It is likely that the developments of the next two decades will be even more dramatic than those of the last two. The ability to distribute information rapidly and inexpensively in electronic form is threatening the entire raison d'être of the library. The library must be evaluated not only in terms of "how it is doing" but also in terms of "is it doing what it should be doing." That is, the library profession must look at its functions critically to determine if it is playing a role appropriate to the last quarter of the twentieth century or one more appropriate to the first quarter.

Evaluation is not an end in itself. An evaluation should be performed only with definite objectives in mind. This will usually mean that a study is designed to answer certain specific questions and to gather data to allow system improvements to be made. An evaluation can be expensive if it is diffuse and lacks well-defined objectives but need not be unreasonably expensive if it is sharply focused. Moreover, the investment made in a careful evaluative study can be fully justified if the results reveal what may need to be done to improve the effectiveness or cost effectiveness of the service or its relevance to the present needs of the community.

Contributors

Patricia Bick, Business Librarian and Economics Bibliographer, has been at the University of Notre Dame since 1976. She is the author of *Business Ethics and Responsibility: An Information Sourcebook* (Oryx Press, 1988).

Christyn Billinsky is an Instructor at the College of Library and Information Science, University of South Carolina, where she has taught since 1979 in the areas of online information services and automated systems in libraries. Before that she served for six years as head of library services at the Charles Stark Draper Laboratory, Inc., Cambridge, Massachusetts.

Susan Bonzi is an Assistant Professor in the School of Information Studies at Syracuse University. She has written in the area of information storage and retrieval in several journals, including *Journal of the American Society for Information Science, Information Processing and Management,* and *Journal of Documentation.*

Michael G. Bowen is an Assistant Professor of Management in the College of Business Administration at the University of Notre Dame. He has published and lectured on topics related to sensemaking and learning issues as they apply to strategic dilemmas. His most recent work examines decisions about whether to recommit resources to questionable or failed courses of action.

John E. Evans has served as head of the Reference and Microforms Department at Memphis State University Libraries since 1981. Previously he held positions as Information Retrieval Specialist and Reference Librarian at MSU and the University of South Dakota. His extensive work with library automation is coupled with his research and publications in the areas of library finance, electronic information retrieval, and the planning and implementation of technology in libraries.

F. Wilfrid Lancaster, Professor of Library and Information Science, University of Illinois, is the author of eight monographs and numerous reports and papers in the field of library/information science. His latest book, *If You Want to Evaluate Your Library,* is published by the Graduate School of Library and Information Science, University of Illinois.

137

Chingkwei Adrienne Lee received her Ph.D. in Linguistics from the University of South Carolina, Columbia, in 1988. Her publications include "Voice Disorder and Speech Therapy" and "New Approach to TEFL: The Functional-Notional Approach," both published in *Journal of National Taichung Institute.* She also published "Phonological Constraints in Uighur" in *Bulletin of the Institute of China Border Area Studies.* Her dissertation is *Information Structure in Planned and Unplanned Discourse.*

John N. Olsgaard, Assistant Dean, College of Library and Information Science, University of South Carolina at Columbia, has published articles in several journals, including *College and Research Libraries, Journal of the American Society of Information Science, Library Journal, Information Technology and Libraries,* and *Journal of Education for Library and Information Science.* He also has upcoming articles that will appear in *Library Trends* and *Journal of Library Administration.*

Carol Tenopir, Associate Professor at the School of Library Information Studies, University of Hawaii, teaches classes in online searching, database design, and information management. She writes the monthly column Online Databases for *Library Journal* and is a frequent contributor to the library literature. She is co-author of *Managing Your Information: How to Design and Create a Textual Database on Your Microcomputer* (Neal-Schuman, 1988).

Danny P. Wallace is an Associate Professor in the Louisiana State University School of Library and Information Science. He has also taught in the library and information science programs of Indiana University and the University of Iowa. He is the author of numerous publications, several of which are bibliometric studies. One of these, "Holdings as a Measure of Journal Value," written with co-author Bert R. Boyce, received the 1988 American Library Association Library Research Round Table Jesse H. Shera Award for Research. The article will appear in a forthcoming issue of *Library and Information Science Research.*

Index